# ERNEST
## Goes To
## Washington

# ERNEST
# Goes To
# Washington
## (Well, not exactly.)

by Al Shugart

**Carmel Bay Publishing Group**
California, USA

Published by Carmel Bay Publishing Group

Permission Department /ML
Carmel Bay Publishing Group
Post Office Box 222543
Carmel, CA 93922-2543 USA

**Library of Congress Cataloging-in-Publication Data**

Catalog No. 98-071606

p. cm.

ISBN: 1-883532-04-3

Photo Credits:
Back cover: Timothy Greenfield-Sanders
Page 38: John Ranallo

Printed in the United States of America

2 4 6 8 10 9 7 5 3

First Edition

# Foreword

I don't know Ernest, but I know Al Shugart, and I wasn't surprised when he tried to get his dog elected to Congress.

Al's a successful businessman and an innovator in the computer technology industry. He's also a maverick. He's always been an independent thinker in his business and in his politics, both of which he feels are too serious not to need a little fun injected into them.

I don't think Ernest will make it in the world of politics—for reasons you'll discover as you read this book. But I think that, like Al, he'll continue to gnaw doggedly at people's funny bones in hopes of getting their attention.

Ernest's run for political office was unsuccessful, but I can offer some consolation: if his efforts inspire more people to take an interest in the political process, they haven't been in vain.

Leon Panetta
Former Chief of Staff
The White House

ERNEST

# Contents

# Introduction

I think the whole Ernest thing got started in the summer of 1995. But my desire to get actively involved in government started a few years before that. Like many people, I had become increasingly disillusioned with the political party system. Congress was getting less and less done, with more and more debate. There was more posturing than ever, more time wasted in committees, and more inter-party sniping.

When Leon Panetta, U.S. Congressman from California's 17th Congressional District, resigned in 1992 to head up the Office of Management and Budget (and ultimately become Chief of Staff in the Clinton administration), I considered running for the seat he'd vacated.

I'd just completed three years of public service as a member of the Board of Governors of NASD (The National Association of Securities Dealers). NASD service required 30 to 40 days a year, and the Board got a lot done. So I believed 40 days each year—maybe a week or so every three months—would be sufficient for Congress to get the job done. To my mind, public service *is* a service, not the pursuit of a perk-driven career.

I discussed the idea with my wife, Rita, and she thought it was an interesting possibility. Unknown to me she even had some campaign buttons made with "Al's Your Pal for Congress" on them. She started

distributing them at our 1992 annual Christmas party. People loved them. I think we had about 120 guests that year, and they all took a button home. My friend Bob Burriss was at the party and he asked if I'd consider making the announcement of my candidacy at the January luncheon of the Carmel Rotary Club, of which he's a member. I said I would if it turned out I was really going to run.

Around the same time my friend Jim McGillen told me he too was thinking about running for Leon's seat. Jim is a real common-sense guy, just the kind of person Congress needs. He and I had one disagreement. It was about how much money would be needed to run a campaign. Jim thought it would take more than a million. I figured about $200,000, max.

I did some reading and studying about Congressional representation and discovered that a Congressman can't hold a second job. That squelched my plan. As CEO of Seagate Technology, a young and growing company, I thought it would be irresponsible to leave and run for public office. But I took comfort in knowing that Jim McGillen was going to run. I was disappointed when I learned in 1993 that Jim had decided not to run. As Jim considered the possibilities for repairing the systemic malfunctioning of Washington, he assessed the chances of a freshman Congressman to effect change. They seemed practically nil, even with two terms. And Jim had no interest in being a career politician.

Between my near-run in 1992 and 1995 when things started heating up for the 1996 elections, the Washington situation didn't improve. In fact it got worse every day. The government continued to put the country in jeopardy. I wondered if there was anybody running without a personal agenda and without a partisan attitude.

I wasn't alone in my feelings. Americans were increasingly disgusted with government. Fewer than 25% of citizens over 18 were going to the polls.

That's when I thought of offering Ernest as a write-in candidate for political office. I wanted to provide a vehicle for voters to express displeasure and get it recorded. Ernest could be the consummate write-in candidate, available for every office. Maybe then the politicians who run things would see how much support they really have (or don't have). I thought it could also spark some interest in people to vote.

Well, I discovered that in the State of California, write-in candidate votes are not counted unless the candidate has been officially declared a legitimate candidate. In California not even "None of the Above" is listed on the ballot; and it won't be counted as a write-in vote, either.

The best course seemed to be to pick one particular contest, and devote whatever attention it took to get Ernest qualified. At least we could get a lot of publicity to build interest in the election, even if we failed to be counted at the end. I picked California's 17th Congressional District as the target; my

district, where I'd considered running for Congress.

A number of questions immediately arose concerning Ernest's candidacy. One in particular—was he constitutionally qualified to serve in Congress? My good friend Jeff Whitmore studied this issue and concluded that all the disqualifying factors mentioned in the United States Constitution related to a "person." Since Ernest wasn't a person, he appeared qualified—or at least he wasn't unqualified outright. However, the requirements in the state of California generally substituted "candidate" for "person," which clouded the issue.

It seemed only a minor snag, so I continued on. Besides, I didn't really think Ernest would get elected. But if his campaign sparked a little more interest and got people more concerned with politics, it would be worthwhile.

When I talked with Rita and some friends about Ernest's candidacy, they all thought it was a good idea. A great idea. They loved it! I discussed the concept with my assistant at Seagate, Karen Seifert, and we went into action. She sent off for the necessary forms, and we did all the required paperwork. Ernest was off and running.

The tale of the paper trail leading back and forth between elections officials and the Friends of Ernest campaign committee is documented in these pages, as well as the extensive and enthusiastic public response to Ernest's candidacy.

Here, then, is the story of Ernest and how he went to Washington. Well, not exactly...

☆ ☆ ☆ ☆ ☆ ☆ ☆ ☆ ☆ ☆ ☆ ☆ ☆

# 1     July 21, 1995

# An Earnest Beginning

The first thing Ernest needed was a Social Security number. So on July 21, 1995, I began the campaign in earnest by applying for his Social Security Card. In completing all the forms for the Social Security Administration, I made no effort to hide the fact that Ernest was a dog. I thought there'd be so many applications that they'd just rubber stamp it and issue a number. I also opted for the San Francisco office, where applications would be far more numerous than in Santa Cruz. Maybe it would slip through there.

They say you get only one chance to make a favorable first impression. No problem. Ernest's lineage and pedigree are impeccable. They couldn't fail to impress. Together with the application form, I included Ernest's American Kennel Club Registration Certificate, which bears his date of birth and the names of his mother, Cita V Taplacs, and his father, Donald Vom Rotelbachtal. Clearly, names of distinction. Ernest applied under his full, official name: Earnest Von Taplacs. I'm not sure when exactly the "a" in "Earnest" was dropped. Probably when he came home as a puppy. We just used the more common spelling—"Ernest."

The Social Security Administration was not impressed. They denied Ernest a Social Security Number. So much for getting a leg up on the very first hurdle.

But Ernest took the setback in stride. He lazed about and slept in the sun as much as before—perhaps resting up for the big campaign yet to come.

During the next couple of months my assistant, Karen Seifert, got "Vote for Ernest" buttons and bumper stickers made. My wife, Rita, took the photos that we used on these. We gave them to friends, business acquaintances, and anybody else who wanted one. The stickers began appearing all around the counties of Santa Cruz and Monterey. Even now, a few cars around town still sport Ernest's photo on their bumpers.

From the beginning, I wanted everything about the campaign to look as professional as possible. At the very least, we needed a nice letterhead. My son, Chris, who's a talented artist, was assigned the task. He conceived a great logo: a dog house bearing Ernest's name superimposed on the Capitol building. It's pretty clever. I decided to call the campaign activities "Friends of Ernest," and that's what figures prominently in red

| 1 | NAME<br>To Be Shown On Card | ▶ EARNEST | VON | TAPLACS |
|---|---|---|---|---|
| | | FIRST | FULL MIDDLE NAME | LAST |

| | FULL NAME AT BIRTH<br>IF OTHER THAN ABOVE | FIRST | FULL MIDDLE NAME | LAST |
|---|---|---|---|---|

OTHER NAMES USED _____

| 2 | MAILING<br>ADDRESS<br>Do Not Abbreviate | ▶ PO BOX 1067 |
|---|---|---|
| | | STREET ADDRESS, APT. NO., PO BOX, RURAL ROUTE NO. |

| PEBBLE BEACH | CA | 93953 |
|---|---|---|
| CITY | STATE | ZIP CODE |

**3 CITIZENSHIP** (Check One)
☒ U.S. Citizen ☐ Legal Alien Allowed To Work ☐ Legal Alien Not Allowed To Work ☐ Foreign Student Allowed Restricted Employment ☐ Conditionally Legalized Alien Allowed To Work ☐ Other (See Instructions On Page 2)

**4 SEX** ☒ Male ☐ Female

**5 RACE/ETHNIC DESCRIPTION** (Check One Only—Voluntary)
☐ Asian, Asian-American Or Pacific Islander ☐ Hispanic ☐ Black (Not Hispanic) ☐ North American Indian Or Alaskan Native ☐ White (Not Hispanic)

| 6 | DATE OF BIRTH | 3-22-93 | 7 | PLACE OF BIRTH | REDDING | CALIF. | | Office Use Only |
|---|---|---|---|---|---|---|---|---|
| | | MONTH DAY YEAR | | (Do Not Abbreviate) | CITY | STATE OR FOREIGN COUNTRY | FCI | |

| 8 | MOTHER'S MAIDEN NAME | CITA | V | TAPLAC'S |
|---|---|---|---|---|
| | | FIRST | FULL MIDDLE NAME | LAST NAME AT HER BIRTH |

| 9 | FATHER'S NAME | DONALD | VOM | ROTELBACHTAL |
|---|---|---|---|---|
| | | FIRST | FULL MIDDLE NAME | LAST |

**10** Has the person in item 1 ever received a Social Security number before?

---

and blue on the letterhead. It was Chris who first observed that the acronym for Friends of Ernest was "FOE." Chris also started work on designing ads for later in January.

•

The first week in September 1995, Karen wrote to the Federal Election Commission and requested the Campaign Guide for Congressional Candidates and Committees and the necessary forms. We finally received them in late January.

I started talking up the campaign at work and among my business and personal friends. Everybody thought it was a great idea. My friend Bob Burriss—who had earlier invited

me to announce my 1992 Congressional bid at the Carmel Rotary Club—now suggested candidate Ernest might announce *his* candidacy there. When Bob discussed it with the club officers, they agreed to have me make the announcement at their January 3, 1996 luncheon. I was really pleased to accept their invitation and looked forward to the event.

The first press mention of Ernest's candidacy was an accident. Early in September I was talking with Herb Greenberg of *The San Francisco Chronicle*. We were discussing a totally different matter and I just happened to mention Ernest's Congressional aspirations. Herb asked if anything had been published about it. I said I didn't think so. So the *Chronicle* was the first to report the news on September 14, 1995.

Herb told the story in his "Business Insider" column:

ERNEST GOES TO WASHINGTON?
*A REAL SHAGGY DOG STORY*
—He's dead serious: Look for a formal announcement in January that Seagate Technology Chairman Al Shugart's 110-pound Bernese mountain dog, Ernest, is running for Congress. Ernest wants to represent the 17th District, which includes Monterey County, Santa Cruz County and part of San Benito County. "He's flawless," Shugart says. "He's not a member of any political party, he has no political experience, he's not a lawyer, he's healthy, he gets no PAC money and he has no debts. He's just perfect for the job." Shugart says Ernest will finance the campaign himself—from a trust fund "that handles this kind of thing." The only

possible catch is that Ernest is just 2-years-old (14 in dog years), and federal law stipulates that Congressional candidates must be at least 25 years old.

Shortly after Greenberg's article appeared, Marin High School students reprinted the story in their "Animal Chronicles" and included a photo of Ernest.

Then, the *San Jose Mercury News* Sunday Perspective Section followed with this report:

Al Shugart, the chairman and CEO of Seagate Technology Inc. of Scotts Valley, may not be a politician's best friend. But it's fair to say he wants to clarify the muddle of elections with—who else—man's best friend. Disturbed that voters were not given a choice of "none of the above," Shugart conceived the idea of a universal write-in candidate who could symbolize voters'

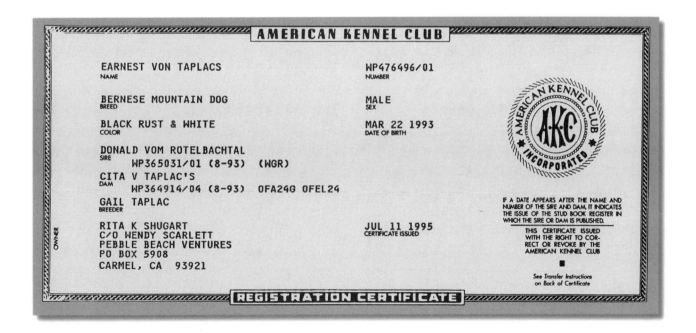

protest. Who did he nominate for this honor? His dog, Ernest, a Bernese mountain dog. Shugart argues that the vote for Ernest could help measure the acceptability of the regular candidates. The Seagate CEO even had a lawyer research how Ernest could get on the ballot. Alas, the attorney found that Monterey authorities would not count votes for Ernest unless he were a qualified write-in. (In most jurisdictions, this takes a declaration and often signatures.) "I was shocked to discover that writing in somebody's name had to be qualified," Shugart told our political editor Phil Trounstine. Shugart says authorities say the dog would have to become a registered voter to qualify. "Ernest is going to have to become human in order to do that," said Santa Clara County Registrar Dwight Beattie.

News of Ernest's campaign spread throughout the technology industry. In a September 25 letter to me, Richard J. Egan, Chairman of the Board of EMC of Massachusetts asked me to pass on to Ernest his appreciation of the candidate's commitment to improving our country's political system. He also wanted Ernest to know he could count on his support.

Several weeks later Dick Egan's support came in the form of a $1,000 check for Friends of Ernest. I thought that was really great. Dick even enclosed his address and Social Security number, so we could properly report his contribution to the Federal Election Commission.

In less than two weeks, news of Ernest's campaign spread nationwide. The internet produced a number of supportive responses.

Among these was one from Carl A. Pick, Chairman of Genroco, Inc., in Wisconsin. He wired his message: "My two year-old mastiff, Hamilton, will throw his weight (210 lbs) behind Ernest's campaign.

I responded via the net: "Thank Hamilton for his heavy support."

•

A campaign fund was the next issue to address. I knew we'd have to set up a special fund to pay for the buttons, bumper stickers, ads, and other campaign expenses. I'd planned to finance the whole campaign myself, and only thought of fund-raising as a way to get publicity. I didn't expect any significant donations.

In early October I opened a non-interest-bearing account at the Coast Commercial Bank in the name of Friends of Ernest. I didn't want to have to bother about reporting interest to the Federal Election Commission, or forgetting to report it. It was set up so that either Karen Seifert, or I could sign. I wrote checks from my personal account to the Friends of Ernest account, and we kept track of the donations through Ernest's trust, which was co-mingled with my account. Rita and I were the trust executors. Money in the trust would be used solely to support the candidacy of animals for public office or in support of the SPCA or a similar animal group whose purpose was to help animals.

The pace of the campaign was starting to pick up. Early in November the week-long International Computer Technology Show (Comdex) was held in Las Vegas. It's a yearly gathering of tens of thousands of people involved in, or interested in, developments in computer technology. Seagate always hosts a hospitality suite during the show.

Ernest figured prominently at Comdex 1995. Cyndy Davis, one of my wife's friends, joined the Seagate group at the suite one evening and was delighted to support Ernest's cause. She mingled with the visitors, giving out "Vote for Ernest" buttons and talking up the campaign. She was a terrific campaigner. About thirty people from all over—the Mid-West, the East Coast, and as far away as England and Brazil—donated to the campaign. We raised more than $550 in amounts from $1.00 to $137. (I figured the odd sum of $137 probably represented someone's earnings at a casino Blackjack table.)

Participants at the show really responded to the concept of a dog running for Congress. Their feedback was great and we had a lot of fun. The "Vote for Ernest" buttons worn around the exhibition hall generated a lot of interest—and laughs!

In his November 20 "Business Insider" column, Herb Greenberg reported on the event:

> Comdex, schmomdex: Seagate CEO Al Shugart just back from the Comdex computer show in Las Vegas, says the most exciting thing that happened was that he raised $551 for his 110-pound Bermese mountain dog, Ernest, who is running for the 17th Congressional district. Shugart says the dog's candidacy, first mentioned here a few months ago, is on track for a formal January launch. Campaign buttons have already been printed,

and a few weeks ago Ernest received a $1,000 contribution from EMC Corp. Chairman Richard Egan. Ernest, incidentally, has competition in the political arena. Abram Still, from Sonora, is running his daughter's Rottweiler, Graffin, for president.

When I learned that Abe's daughter's Rottweiler was a presidential candidate, I sent him a campaign button and a write-up about Ernest. I felt sure he'd like to know more about a fellow canine candidate.

After Herb Greenberg's earlier report about Ernest, *San Jose Mercury News* reporter Tracie Cone called me. She wanted to do a feature for the paper's Sunday *West* magazine. Ernest and I were delighted. She interviewed us and wrote an excellent article featuring Ernest's photo for the November 19, 1995 issue.

IN DOG WE TRUST

What Congress needs, computer magnate Al Shugart figures, is someone Ernest, someone who will follow his or her instincts and do what is right, regardless of race, breed, political affiliation, or pedigree.

Shugart's perfect candidate would give paws for reflection in that dog-eat-dog House of Representatives, and perhaps force members to sit up and take notice before this country goes to the—Ack! Stop me before I get caught up in this Ernest-for-Congress thing that has seemingly turned a successful corporate CEO into someone who sounds like just another California flake.

Ernest is a dog who happens to live with the president of Seagate Technology, who happens to think our country's gravy train has derailed and the current crop of partisan politicians is the reason. So Shugart has decided to spend as much as it takes of his own considerable savings promoting Ernest as a viable alternative candidate to human Sam Farr in the 17th Congressional District, which covers much of Monterey and Santa Cruz counties.

"He's a good dog," Shugart says of Ernest. "Also, he's not a lawyer."

Which are two things that can't be said about most folks in politics, except maybe Al Gore.

Shugart decided to attempt to put Ernest on the ballot after becoming consumed by the prevailing feeling of exasperation with all things government, especially federal. When he looked around and assessed who was running the country, Shugart decided that the creature who maintained order in his Pebble Beach back yard was equally adept.

"I have no confidence in the president, or Congress or anyone in government," says Shugart, who splits his time as chairman of both the board of his computer company and Friends of Ernest, the campaign committee. "We have to dismantle it and start over, and voting for Ernest would send that message."

(Farr's people, by the way, did not respond to requests for comment about his furry foe, deferring to John Laird, chairman

Become a **FOE** (Friend of Ernest)

of the Santa Cruz Democratic Party, who called to say: "I hope this isn't just another corporate lap dog. Something smells about this whole thing.!")

Ernest has developed a campaign platform. He communicated it telepathically to Shugart, who, despite telling people that this is the manner by which Ernest has outlined his four-legged stand, still does not occupy a padded room, possibly because he makes more money than we do. Rich people can be eccentric, the rest of us are crazy.

"He got pretty specific on some of his stands," says Shugart. "He told me, 'We have to eliminate the subpoena power of the IRS.' Now how did he know that?"

Shugart and his assistant have been researching how to get Ernest on the November '96 ballot for months. The effort has been futile so far; our founding fathers probably did not foresee a time when multimillionaires would run their animal companions for national office. The fact that Shugart can find no one to give him answers has shown the campaign team that now, more than ever, it is time for government to be more responsive to all creatures.

"We haven't gotten anything back from the federal government," Shugart says. "The state sent us some stuff, but it was for partisan candidates. Ernest doesn't belong to a political party. We got information on how to file a campaign report, and we still don't know how to get him on the ballot. This process has been very frustrating."

Ernest's best friend, Calvin, a basset hound who is cuter that Ernest but is content to work out of the limelight, is the campaign treasurer. Calvin approves all campaign expenses (telepathically, of course) like the full-page newspaper ads that will debut when the candidate formally announces Jan. 3 at the Carmel Rotary Club meeting, where Sam Farr's dad, retired state Sen. Fred Farr, is a member, and, presumably, won't be jumping on the Ernest-for-Congress bandwagon. Until then, Friends of Ernest is handing out buttons and Post-it notes with Ernest's fuzzy face superimposed over an American flag.

There are, of course, some obvious problems with 2-year-old Ernest's candidacy. To run for Congress, one must be 25. Shugart believes that age applies to people only. Ernest, though 14 in human years, may be a tad young to qualify for the ballot. On the plus side, Ernest is a natural-born American. Even though he is called a Bernese mountain dog, Ernest has never actually been to Berne, Switzerland, the land of his ancestors and, I believe, would not necessarily enact laws favoring the Swiss. In fact, Shugart says Ernest has no loyalties whatsoever, beyond being a faithful companion and adequate watch dog, which is all we want from a politician anyway.

"If he's elected, it would be a terrible tragedy," says Shugart, "but it could happen in Santa Cruz."

In a distinguished hall that already has housed a Gopher (Fred "Gopher" Grandy, R-Iowa, formerly on "The Love Boat" TV show) Ernest might not cause much of a fuss. Something that could make Ernest stand out in the pack, however, is his canine way of greeting new friends by sniffing a point on the backside of their anatomies—and you can't say that about most politicians. Or can you?

Perhaps Ernest instinctively knows how to behave in Washington. And after retirement, he would make a swell lobbyist.

Following the publication of Tracie's article I received over twenty calls and letters about it. The response to her piece was so broad and enthusiastic, that it gave me the idea to do a book about Ernest's campaign. The book would include letters people wrote to Ernest, as well as the media reaction to his candidacy. Tracie is such a witty and talented writer, I thought she'd be the right person to put it all together. Her agent and I discussed the proposal, but they decided against it; it wasn't the right time for her to commit to the book.

Herb Greenberg, continued to get responses about Ernest from his "Business Insider" column. He wrote on November 21:

—Regarding yesterday's column on the political aspirations of Seagate Technology Chairman Al Shugart's "Bermese" mountain dog, Ernest, David Rowland writes: "It's BERNESE, as in Berne, Switzerland. We have a 5-year-old male named Buster. He has no political aspirations."

☆ ☆ ☆ ☆ ☆ ☆ ☆ ☆ ☆ ☆ ☆ ☆ ☆

# 2 November 22, 1995

# A Mandate From The People– And The Animals

On November 22, we received the first of many letters "written" by animals. Two little dogs started it off. Barbara Sullivan, their "human," as the canines called her, obviously has a great sense of humor. I laughed when I read the letter "signed" with their paw prints:

*We are two alums of the Santa Clara County Humane Society, rescued years ago by a very kind, loving human who has proven to be eminently "trainable!" (For example, she is writing this letter for us.)*

*We were shown the article in Sunday's paper entitled, "In Dog We Trust" and were so excited we immediately adjourned to the back yard to hurl barks and invectives at the neighbor's stupid cat!!! (Who thinks she's "hot stuff" because of you-know-who in the White House!)*

*We would willingly contribute all our dog biscuits to Ernest's campaign but our human explained that newspapers prefer coin of "their realm" instead for ads and things. However, our human has agreed to ask for two campaign buttons (Does Calvin have a button?) and send you whatever coins they cost. We would proudly wear them on our collars when we're out for our walks and share this "good news" with everyone at the park. Our human has said some very nasty things about Congress…especially during the 6:00 PM news…so I think we could safely say she would vote for Ernest but for the fact that she lives in the wrong county. We understand that there are a number of "dogs" already there, so he should feel right at home.*

*Please give Ernest our best wishes. He looks like a true "leader of men" and dominator of cats! We are truly proud of him and think he rates a 21-woof salute!!!*

*Mandy (Toy dachshund representing senior doggies) and Fritz (a veritable melting pot representing all cat chasers and guardians of food bowls)*

Of course I sent two campaign buttons right away.

A second letter arrived the same day from Guy Jinkerson, one of my attorney friends in San Jose:

*Dear Al:*

*I read with great interest the article about your dog Ernest in the* West Magazine *for November 19, 1995. I consider myself an independent thinker and I am always willing to consider new ideas. However, before I can support Ernest's campaign for Congress I need to know a few things:*

*1. Does Ernest drink VO and water?*
*2. Can he fish?*
*3. Can he bark the words final, final, final?*
*4. Will he accept contributions from a lawyer?*
*5. Is Ernest interested in legal endorsements? My former colleague from the Public Defender's Office, Rose Bird, has not had a lot to do for the past nine years and she may be available to endorse Ernest.*

*I look forward to hearing from you soon so that I can determine if I may be of assistance in this important campaign.*

I attempted to match his humor with my response:

*Dear Guy,*

*While Ernest certainly drinks a lot of water, I don't believe he has ever tried VO. In fact, I don't believe he has ever drunk any alcoholic beverage; not necessarily a moral or religious issue, but rather an availability issue.*

*Ernest has never fished, but is anxiously awaiting completion of our koi pool so he can find out if he can do it.*

*Ernest doesn't bark too much, and seldom in English. Also, Ernest is not a quitter, so he may not ever use the word "final."*

*As for accepting contributions from a lawyer, Ernest likes to quote Reverend Billy Sunday who said, "The devil's money can do the work of God."*

*As of now, Ernest expects to make a formal announcement of his candidacy on January 3. Following that announcement, newspaper advertisements, and hopefully an appearance on* Larry King Live, *I'm sure he will be interested in drumming up any support he can get.*

The letters continued to come in. There was one from a little cocker spaniel who wanted to wear an Ernest button on his collar. We began sending buttons to all who wrote us—dog, cat, or person. All these letters were such fun to read that I decided to keep them in an "Ernest" file.

News about Ernest traveled across the country via the internet. I received a message from Marianne Becktel in Michigan, who suggested a campaign "at the REAL grass root level"—that being the place where dogs live their lives. Marianne wrote that she raises Bernese Mountain Dogs and suggested featuring Ernest in a specialty magazine geared exclusively to the breed. I had no idea that Bernese Mountain Dogs had their own publication.

She had this advice for me:

*Dear Al,*

*Why not give Ernest that big boost by campaigning with "His Own?" There are nearly 400 Bernese folk worldwide on the Bernese mailing list who would love to hear his platform, and may even have some strategic suggestions for him! And, noteworthy as he is, I am sure [we] could find a place on the Bernese Mountain Dog Home Page for him. And of course, Ernest should make an appearance at the Bernese Mountain Dog Specialty Show which happens to be next April in San Francisco!*

Unfortunately, we couldn't commit yet to Ernest's attending the Bernese Mountain Dog Specialty Show in April. My heavy travel schedule for Seagate had to come first. But we did send some buttons and information to Marianne and the Bernese Mountain Dog specialty people.

*The Business Journal,* a newspaper serving San Jose and Silicon Valley, caught the Ernest contagion. Michelle Hosteller interviewed me and then wrote, in the December 3 issue:

TECH EXECS GIVE DOG CANDIDATE
A FEW BONES

Ernest, the dog belonging to Al Shugart, the indomitable chief executive of Seagate Technology, is drumming up campaign contributions in his quest for the 17th Congressional District seat.

As of last week, Ernest had raised $2,051 to fund his race against incumbent Sam Farr, D-Carmel, a human.

The district encompasses much of Monterey and Santa Cruz counties. A $500 check arrived in the mail Nov. 20 for Friends of Ernest from John Adler, chairman of Adaptec Inc. in Milpitas, said Mr. Shugart.

Much of the other $1,551 is rumored to have come from executives with Komag Inc. and Read-Rite Corp. The money is being used to produce buttons and other campaign items.

A 2-year-old Bernese mountain pure breed, Ernest is not dogmatic in his political stands. He communicates telepathically with Mr. Shugart at their Pebble Beach home, informing his master of his beliefs—for example, that the IRS's subpoena power should be eliminated.

The political wag's furry ambitions were unveiled by the San Jose Mercury News in a West magazine piece Nov. 19. Ernest likes the article but is upset that the writer said his pal, a basset hound named Calvin, is cuter than he is, Mr. Shugart said.

My good friend John Adler of Adaptec sent his hefty $500 check to Ernest "to boost his luck." It was second only to Dick Egan's whopping $1,000, which I mentioned earlier. The pot was growing. By mid-December we'd raised over $4,000. Although I had talked to both John and Dick by phone, I thanked them in writing when we got our official Friends of Ernest stationery. I told them I hadn't even paid out any money yet, and the reason: "The button guy hasn't even sent us a bill." I made sure to enclose the *West* magazine article about Ernest for each of them.

Abe Still, whose daughter and her

presidential candidate Rottweiler were mentioned by Herb Greenberg in his November 20 Business Insider column, wrote to me on December 6:

*Attention: Al Shugart (Ernest's man)*

*Dear Sir:*

*Thank you for Ernest's campaign button and the accompanying flyer. As you are aware, I am running my daughter's dog, Graffin, as a nonpartisan candidate for President of the United States. Graffin would deeply appreciate any information you have prepared on Ernest's political objectives, other than getting elected. That, naturally, is a candidate's first order of business…and sometimes it seems, the only one. Graffin's campaign is strictly issue-oriented and to date has been conducted solely through letters to the editor in Sonora's* Union Democrat. *He would be happy to send Ernest, for his consideration, copies of the positions he has taken on a number of subjects. Graffin believes it would be a good thing if there were a K9 candidate for the U.S. Senate. Could this by any chance be Calvin?*

*Yours for a Dog Gone Better Country,*

*Abe Still*

I gave Abe an honest answer about candidate Ernest and Calvin in my December 11 letter:

*Dear Abe,*

*Thanks for the letter.*

*Ernest has no political objectives beyond getting elected and promoting his sense of values. His most frequent position is lying down. And Calvin has not displayed a lot of interest in the campaign or politics in general, forcing us to appoint an Assistant Treasurer.*

*Regards,*

*Al Shugart*

My sister, Margaret Shugart Kraght, who is an animal-lover and accomplished amateur photographer of butterflies, has designed her letterhead to read, "*KRAGHT HAVEN*, Home for Wayward Cats." On December 2 she wrote from Kraght Haven to let us know that word about Ernest had spread to Southern California:

*Dear Friends:*

*We, too, are Friends of Ernest, having met him on visits to the Shugart menagerie in Pebble Beach. A mutual friend gave us a flyer advertising Ernest's candidacy, and we must say it sounds great. We are circulating it among our friends in this area, who share our enthusiasm; and if Ernest goes on to run for Senator at some later date, we can guarantee a good bloc of votes from the San Gabriel Valley. We hope that won't be too long, for most of our friends are elderly people in nursing homes, and you know how that goes. But they really love dogs and cats and are fervent boosters of Ernest's candidacy. Which brings up another item: the Ernest campaign buttons.*

*I'd dearly love to have one of these, both to wear during this campaign, sharing the word with all who see it, and to add to my collection of campaign buttons. This fine collection (most of it inherited from my mother) includes a Willkie button (of course!), and buttons for Rockefeller, Landon, Knowland, Kennedy, Nixon, Ike & Nixon, Goldwater, Coolidge, Hoover, Roosevelt, and a button proclaiming "I don't want Eleanor either." (You can see my mother was a Republican.) In addition, I have a nice one advising "VOTE NO ON YES" and another advocating "NOBODY FOR PRESIDENT." So you can see, not only would Ernest be in famous company, he would also provide needed balance.*

*Now that we have a cat in the White House, what's more logical than a dog in Congress? I'll bet Ernest is as good on rat control as Socks is, and you know how many rats there are in Washington.*

*Please send me a button, and give Ernest an encouraging pat on the back from all of us at Kraght Haven!*

I responded promptly:

*Dear Margaret,*

*Too bad you can't vote for Ernest, but we are enclosing some stuff anyway. (Two buttons; one to preserve in your collection and one to wear.) We'll try to keep you posted if the campaign treasury doesn't run out of stamp money, and if Calvin doesn't run off with the dough.*

•

With declaration day just a few weeks off, I wanted to be sure everything was on track for Ernest's big announcement. I wrote to the Registrar of Voters for Monterey County.

Though the response from Tony Achundo, the Registrar of Voters, was prompt, the information didn't seem to be in Ernest's favor. Mr. Achundo's letter, in effect, implied that Ernest's eligibility was at best, highly questionable.

We definitely had another hurdle to face, but that wouldn't stall the campaign.

# Friends of Ernest

December 14, 1995

Registrar of Voters
P.O. Box 1848
Salinas, CA 93902-1848

Dear Registrar of Voters,

I need some clarification of your Voter Information with respect to age.

Ernest, a soon to be announced candidate for the U.S. Congress from California's 17th District, would like to register to vote in Monterey County. The Voter Information states that 18 years is the minimum age. This seems to be in conflict with the laws governing election to Congress, in that these federal positions require a minimum age for "persons."  Since Ernest is a dog, and not a "person," this federal law is not applicable.

Please advise if the voter registration minimum age applies to "persons" only. If this is not the case, is it satisfactory to use one dog year equals seven human years.

Thank you for your help.

Regards,

Alan F. Shugart

Friends of Ernest • PO Box 5908 • Carmel • CA 93921 • Treasurer: Calvin

# MONTEREY COUNTY

## ELECTION DEPARTMENT
P.O. BOX 1848, 93902 - 1370 B SOUTH MAIN STREET, SALINAS, CALIFORNIA 93901

**TONY ANCHUNDO**
REGISTRAR OF VOTERS

| 755-5085 | SALINAS |
| 647-7621 | MONTEREY |
| 385-8321 | KING CITY |
| 755-5485 | FAX |

**JUNEL DAVIDSEN**
ASSISTANT REGISTRAR OF VOTERS

December 19, 1995

Alan Shugart
PO Box 5908
Carmel CA 93921

Subject: Requirements for House of Representatives, U.S. Congress

The Constitution of the United States specifies qualifications for election to the House of Representatives. A Representative must be a person who is at least twenty five years of age, and who has been a citizen of the United States for at least seven years and who is a resident of the State being represented. There are no provisions for other kinds of representation.

In addition, the California Elections Code provides for voter registration with political party affiliation as specified. Please see enclosures for state filing requirements including execution of a Declaration of Candidacy.

California Elections Code Section #2000 provides that a voter must be a person at least 18 years of age. This follows the 26th Amendment to the Constitution of the United States in 1971 which lowered the voting age to eighteen years. The minimum age is applicable to persons because only persons may be registered to vote.

Therefore, a Representative to the United States Congress House of Representatives must be a person meeting the qualifications specified in the U.S. Constitution and meeting the requirements of California State Law.

Please let us know if you have further questions.

Sincerely,

Tony Anchundo, Registrar of Voters
County of Monterey

ENCLOSURES

☆ ☆ ☆ ☆ ☆ ☆ ☆ ☆ ☆ ☆ ☆ ☆ ☆

# 3 | December 13, 1995

# A National Candidate With International Appeal

News of Ernest's campaign reached Europe on December 13, 1995. Two Bernese Mountain Dogs named "Ayscha" and "Benja" "wrote" to tell us about it. Their owners, Claudius and Marita Hogger-Tomorug, from Welver, Germany, summed up their wise assessment of Ernest's candidacy and the American political scene: "We vote for you! Every voice for your aim is important. The country is indifferent."

They enclosed a clipping from their local German newspaper describing in detail the news of Ernest's candidacy. His photograph figured prominently under the caption: *"Ernest—ein Hundeleben als Politiker"* in large letters, and the sub-caption, *"Mit Instinkt und Spurnase: Ein Vierbeiner soll die US—Politik umkrempeln—"kein Anwalt."*

One of Ernest's German shepherd friends translated it for him: "Ernest—A Dog's Life As A Politician—With Instinct And A Good Nose: A Four-Legger Should Turn US Politics Around—Not A Lawyer."

Was Ernest gaining worldwide recognition?

The French also read about "le chien candidat" in December. Emmanuel Vitrac at the Seagate European Corporate Communications Office in Boulogne-Billancourt faxed me a copy of a piece about Ernest that appeared in the December 13 issue of *PC Dealer*, in the "Channel Talk" column:

> CHANNEL TALK IS A FAN OF
> AL SHUGART,
> the off-the-wall president of Seagate. Big Al is not your common or garden variety president. This funky guy rocks the house, as it were. His latest wheeze was at Comdex, where he displayed his disapproval of US politics. He handed out badges for his dog, after nominating the hound to run for California Senator. Fortunately, sense prevailed and Shugart took it upon himself to find Ernest a proper manager who will be less corrupt than usual—he chose his other dog, Higgins.

Despite the inaccuracies, the piece was pretty funny. Ernest however growled a bit about being called a "hound," and Calvin whined about being misnamed "Higgins."

# Ernest – ein Hundeleben als Politiker

## Mit Instinkt und Spürnase: Ein Vierbeiner soll die US-Politik umkrempeln – „Kein Anwalt"

Von C. BIEGLER

**Monterey.** Am 3. Januar wird Ernest seine Kandidatur für den Washingtoner Kongreß erklären. Nein, erklären ist das falsche Wort. Ernest wird seine Pläne für eine politische Karriere kundtun, indem er bellt oder mit dem buschigen Schwanz wedelt.

Für die Vorstellung seiner Wahlplattform hat Ernest einen Dolmetscher. Er heißt Al Shugart und leitet das Wahlkampf-Komitee „Friends of Ernest" (Ernests Freunde). Außerdem ist Shugart Vorsitzender und Präsident einer Firma (Seagate Technologies) im kalifornischen Scotts Valley. Zur Zeit investiert er neben Zeit einen Teil seines – allerdings beträchtlichen – Vermögens in einen Werbefeldzug für seinen Vierbeiner.

Ernest hat nach Ansicht seines Herrchens nicht nur zwei Beine mehr als die derzeitigen Kongreßabgeordneten, sondern auch sonst viele Qualitäten, die den Washingtoner Politikern fehlen. Der Berner Sennenhund sei (wie sein Vorname besagt) ernst. Er folge stets seinem Instinkt und tue, was er für richtig halte – unabhängig von Parteien, Rasse und Stammbaum. Ernest sei klug, treu und besitze eine sensible Spürnase. Vor allem aber: Er wisse, was es bedeute, ein Hundeleben zu führen. Daher sei er wie kein anderer prädestiniert, dem amerikanischen Volk ein ähnliches Schicksal zu ersparen.

„Er ist ein guter Hund", sagt Shugart. „Und er ist kein Anwalt." Von dieser Sorte Mensch gibt es nach Ansicht des Unternehmers in der Washingtoner Politik ohnehin „viel zu viele".

Shugart will mit der Kandidatur seines Vierbeiners auf die Mißstände in den USA aufmerksam machen. Ohne Humor, sagt der Unternehmer, sähe alles noch düsterer aus. Buttons mit dem zotteligen Kopf des Kongreßabgeordneten in spe und der US-Flagge im Hintergrund sind bereits im Umlauf, und auf Flugblättern werden Ernests Qualitäten gepriesen. Wenn der Hund am 3. Januar in der Stadt Carmel den zweibeinigen Demokraten Sam Farr im 17. Wahldistrikt mit den Bezirken Monterey und Santa Cruz offiziell herausfordert, sollen in mehreren Zeitungen ganzseitige Anzeigen erscheinen.

Bassett Calvin, als Ernests bester Freund von Shugart zum Schatzmeister des Wahlkampf-Ausschusses erkoren, hat neben den Ressourcen des Computer-Magnaten auch mehrere tausend Dollar an Spenden in seinen Pfoten.

Jeder in den USA hat das Recht, seine Kandidatur für ein politisches Amt zu erklären. Aber um schließlich auf dem Wahlzettel aufzutauchen, muß man einige Voraussetzungen erfüllen. So kann niemand unter 25 Jahren in den Kongreß gewählt werden. Ernest zählt zwei Lenze, was 14 Menschenjahren entspricht. Aber dieses Manko kümmert Shugart wenig. Die Regeln, so argumentiert er, seien für Menschen gemacht. Nirgendwo stehe geschrieben, daß sie auch für Hunde gelten.

**ECHT TIERISCH:** Sennenhund „Ernest" soll US-Politik umkrempeln.          Foto: dpa

Sometimes they're touchy about those kinds of things.

•

Around this time Congress was considering a Securities litigation bill which would make it tougher to bring class action suits in federal court. The President vetoed the bill. In their December 22, 1995 vote, however, Congress overturned his veto. Congress was solidly behind passage of the Law. As campaign chairman for Ernest's campaign, it was important to let the President know where we stood. So on December 22 I wrote him a letter explaining our position.

A couple days earlier I had a phone call from the Carmel Rotary Club Program Director, Bob Burriss, regarding the invitation that had been extended to Ernest to formally announce his candidacy at the January 3, 1996 meeting of the club. Bob told me the invitation had been withdrawn. I was really disappointed. I had looked forward to the opportunity to announce Ernest's candidacy at the club luncheon.

# Friends of Ernest

December 22, 1995

Vance Baldwin
President
Carmel Rotary Club
P.O. Box 774
Carmel, CA 93921

Dear Vance,

Ernest was saddened when I told him we had been dis-invited to the January 3 Carmel Rotary Club luncheon. He wasn't so sad to miss the luncheon (I don't think he really wanted to go anyway), but rather to find supposed leaders of our community unclear on the concept of protesting the way our government works (or doesn't work) and even more significant, the absence of a sense of humor.

Calvin was surprised also, suggesting that perhaps I had been misinformed, and that it was really a Bar Association meeting (I think Calvin's been listening to me or had a bad tort experience).

Ernest's announcement is still planned for January 3 with a release to major newspapers and wire services worldwide. You can expect to see advertisements in Monterey and Santa Cruz County newspapers on January 11.

Regards,

Alan F. Shugart
Campaign Chairman

enclosure

I never got an explanation.

On January 3, 1996, the day we were to have made our formal announcement at the Carmel Rotary Club we sent a press release to *The Monterey County Herald*, *The Carmel Pine Cone*, *Coast Weekly*, *The Santa Cruz County Sentinel*, *Good Times* of Santa Cruz, and to wire services worldwide.

After this first press release I thought it would be good to continue releasing information to the media to keep the public informed about the progress of Ernest's campaign. Julie Still, who manages our Seagate Corporate Communications office, helped a lot with the writing of these news releases.

We made sure that Ernest and Calvin never really said or spoke words directly. It was always "dog talk." They might "convey," growl, or bark, or even "whine" something (Calvin whines sometimes, Ernest never does.)

# Friends of Ernest

## PRESS RELEASE

*For Immediate Release*
Contact: Al Shugart
(408) 439-2244

### ERNEST CALLS FOR BOLD LEADERSHIP, COMMON SENSE
### IN BID FOR CONGRESSIONAL SEAT
*Finally, an Ernest Candidate, Say Supporters*

Carmel, Calif., January 3, 1996 — Promising bold new leadership for the people of California's 17th District, and a commitment to common sense in government, better schools, more trees on the streets and an environment free from frivolous lawsuits, Ernest today announced his candidacy for U.S. Congress.

"The choice in this election is about leadership and common sense. Our streets are losing their appeal, our schools are going to the dogs, and lawsuits are ruining free enterprise and the American dream. It's time for a change," Ernest conveyed to a pack of supporters outside of the Carmel Rotary Club luncheon here. Two weeks earlier, the Rotary Club disinvited Ernest, who was scheduled to announce his candidacy at the club's meeting.

Ernest, a resident of Pebble Beach, Calif., went on to thank his supporters and outline his vision of a no-nonsense, apolitical national government by pointing out the people, issues, and spirit that have shaped his views.

"He's flawless. He's not a member of an ordinary political party, he has no political experience, he's not a lawyer, he's healthy, he gets no PAC money and he has no debts. He's just perfect for the job," said Al Shugart, Seagate Technology's Chairman, and the Congressional candidate's campaign chairman. "He's proven himself in this dog-eat-dog world as the only candidate capable of addressing the concerns of the American people."

The campaign is being financed by Ernest, from a trust fund "that handles this sort of thing," and supporters of the Friends of Ernest (FOE) campaign committee, headquartered in Carmel, Calif.

Ernest feels the promise of strong leadership and common sense is the only way to rid Congress of Democrats and Republicans alike. It is time for common sense to reign once again.

As a member of Congress, Ernest wants to help lead the way to a revival, not only of his District's fortunes, but of the unique spirit of America that is rooted in common sense, freedom and the pursuit of happiness.

☆ ☆ ☆ ☆ ☆ ☆ ☆ ☆ ☆ ☆ ☆ ☆ ☆

# 4 January 11, 1996

# The Campaign Is Launched

We planned a major follow-up to the January 3 announcement: a full-page ad to be published simultaneously in four local newspapers on January 11. Chris, my son, designed a great-looking ad. (The ads, we discovered, were really expensive, but I believed we needed the impact of the full page to make a serious statement about the state of the American political system.)

Chris contacted the ad department of each paper to arrange placement of the ad. It was interesting that *The Santa Cruz Sentinel* offered a discount for a political ad, whereas the *Monterey County Herald* imposed an additional charge. (I'm still not sure how political advertising rates are calculated.)

Even more interesting was the fact that the *Herald* wanted us to make a slight change in our ad copy. For reasons unknown, they were uneasy about the last line at the bottom of the ad. It read, "This advertisement paid for by Friends of Ernest." This was not considered sufficient, even though the ad department had already accepted the ad—with a smile and a laugh. The ad rep said the editorial department wanted the name of a person to appear in the ad.

When Chris reported this to me, he said it would be easy to change the copy. In fact, he said the *Herald* would gladly do it at no extra cost and without any further delays.

I didn't even have to think about my response. I insisted the ad should run as is or not at all. When Chris relayed this back to the ad department, the ad rep said he'd be more than happy to run the ad as it was. After all, they'd received the art work complete, and a check for the full amount. But he said he'd have to clear it with management.

The next day he called Chris and said that the ad department manager would handle the situation, and assured Chris there wouldn't be a problem. All seemed well. That is, until the day before the ad was supposed to appear. On that day, Chris received a phone call at 4 P.M.—one hour before the deadline. A very apologetic ad rep said that Susan Miller, the *Herald* president and editor, was still unwilling to run the ad without the addition of a name (a human one).

Chris said that our position hadn't changed. Run the ad as is or return the money.

The ad rep could make no promises, but he said he was willing to have one more go at it.

# Let's Send Ernest to Washington!

The political system is broken, which prevents all our broken government systems from being fixed.
The problems are too great to be left to politicians.
***The country is going to the dogs!***

## HERE IS OUR CHANCE FOR THE ULTIMATE PROTEST!

# VOTE FOR ERNEST

**For U.S. Representative from California's 17th District**

ERNEST

*A Clear Vision of Values Based upon*
*Fairness, Honesty, Ethics, and Common Sense*

☆ NO PAC MONEY
☆ NO DEBTS
☆ NO POLITICAL EXPERIENCE
☆ NOT A LAWYER

☆ HEALTHY
☆ INTELLIGENT
☆ FRIENDLY
☆ HOUSE BROKEN

This advertisement paid for by
*Friends of Ernest.*

PO Box 5908, Carmel, CA 93921

Treasurer: Calvin

The matter effectively ended there. If the ad rep was successful, we'd see the ad next morning. If not, the $2,800 check would have to be returned. Despite all the back-and-forth hassle, the ad appeared the next day—exactly as we had submitted it!

•

Four more letters of support arrived for Ernest between the January 3rd article and the January 11 advertisement. One of the cleverest pledges of support came from "Red Dog," a magnificent sporting dog, who sent us his handsome photograph and his very own personal check. The check looked pretty real, but I don't think I ever tried to cash it.

On the same day the full-page ad appeared, The *Herald* carried this story by *Herald* staff writer, Joe Livernois:

### ADS PROMOTE DOG AS CANDIDATE FOR CONGRESS

Ernest might never get elected dogcatcher, but he's begging to be a candidate for the 17th Congressional District.

Ernest is a dog. A Bernese mountain dog, to be exact.

Full-page advertisements urging readers to "Vote for Ernest" appear today in the *Herald*, as well as in the *Santa Cruz Sentinel*, the *Carmel Pine Cone* and the *Good Times* in Santa Cruz.

How much is that? Well, the *Herald* ad cost $2800—the political rate plus a premium for placement in the main news section, Advertising Director Jay Palmquist said.

"Here is your chance for the ultimate

protest!" proclaims the ad, which includes a handsome photograph of Ernest himself and a list of qualifications that includes "healthy, intelligent, friendly, not a lawyer" and, more important, "house broken."

The ad doesn't mention whether Ernest can beg. Or roll over. Or if he knows the difference between a budget compromise and a soup bone.

Ernest is owned by Pebble Beach resident Alan Shugart, chairman of Seagate Technology Inc. of Scotts Valley, one of the world's leading producers of computer disk drives.

Shugart identified himself yesterday as Ernest's campaign manager. The ad identifies a basset hound named Calvin as the campaign treasurer.

A spokeswoman for the Monterey County Election Office said Ernest is barking up the wrong tree. Ernest missed the official deadline to file for the March election.

And technically, a dog can't run for any public office, even if it's been licensed and had its shots. Write-ins for Ernest won't be counted.

Shugart said Ernest's campaign is based on the premise "that common sense is the only way to rid Congress of Democrats and Republicans alike."

But the ad is obviously Shugart's statement on the state of the nation. "The political system is broken," he said, "which prevents all our broken government systems from being fixed. The problems are too great to be left to politicians. The country is going to the dogs."

Through Associated Press wire services, Livernois's article was also published in *The Houston Chronicle* on January 12, and *The Milwaukee Journal Sentinel* on January 14 under the caption, "This Candidate's Not Above Begging For Public Office: Dog Named Ernest Touted For California House Seat."

Once the newspapers broke the news of Ernest's candidacy, local TV and radio media reported the story. KSBW and KCCN TV aired segments about Ernest on the January 8 evening news.

Anchorperson Dina Ruiz, who reported the story for KSBW, (together with the rest of the news team) displayed her button and bumper sticker with obvious enjoyment.

KCCN's Cornell Barnard interviewed me at my home. Cornell had fun trying to interview Calvin, who snorted noisily into his microphone. When Ernest just wagged his tail and let his tongue hang out the side of his mouth, Cornell commented, "He certainly won't give in to demands from the press!"

Publication of the political ad prompted another TV report on KNTV, San Jose on January 11.

The KNTV reporter concluded the segment with a reference to Ernest's good looks: "Since the country's going to the dogs, why not elect Ernest to take it there in style!"

KCBA of Salinas, not wanting to be left out, but finding me and Ernest unavailable, ended up interviewing Chris. He was the only spokesperson they could find on short notice.

The KCBA reporter began his report: "This guy's got some bite to him." I think he was referring to Ernest.

Also on January 11, Darryl Allen Gault,

who hosts Santa Cruz radio station KSCO's "Daily Rail," interviewed us by phone. Gault laughed heartily throughout our conversation. He mentioned that one caller during the previous day's show wanted to know if the point of Ernest's candidacy was that we should have "None of the Above" or a write-in category on the election ballot.

Once again I responded that our purpose was to alert people that our political system has been broken by lawyers, both Republicans and Democrats. Also the campaign was supposed to be a protest. I added that we don't get a chance to vote on all the "committees" that essentially keep the government from doing anything really worthwhile.

Gault commented that "most of that is driven by special interests, and that needs to be curbed." I concurred and reiterated the point of Ernest's candidacy was to offer a flag, a rallying point around which the deep dissatisfaction of the people can coalesce. If people become aware of the systemic disaster our government has become, they will take action and demand that it be fixed.

Gault asked about Ernest's position on a number of issues, such as allowing cats into government positions, more trees on the streets, the remodeling of fire hydrants, taxes, mortgage deductions on dog houses, leash laws, the budget. We had a lot of fun and a lot of agreement about the need for government reform *now* and the need for balancing the budget this year instead of in seven years.

•

Newspaper, TV and radio exposure during the month of January prompted forty-two letters and postcards. Some were addressed to Ernest, some to Calvin, others to me or to Friends of Ernest. A dozen of the letters included contributions ranging from one dollar to twenty-five dollars. A few writers included photographs of dogs, cats, and children. Some people sent dog bones, dog treats, etc. Someone sent us "doggie bucks," which looked like some sort of canine currency—perhaps the kind of money that dogs use. Everyone pledged enthusiastic support. People and dogs alike were eager to offer their services as assistant campaign manager, secretary, staff member, speechwriter, publicity manager. There were even cats who abandoned their ancient antipathies in support of Ernest.

During the weeks following the full-page advertisement and *Herald* article, a number

10 Doggie Bucks

*Ernest for Office*

10 Doggie Bucks

Treasurer: Calvin the Basset

of Letters to the Editor appeared in some of the local newspapers.

## APPRECIATES AD

Thank you, Alan Shugart, for your foresight in placing the ad to send Ernest to Washington. You made my day! I have framed the whole page as a constant reminder of how much help we really need in the nation's capital.

My only suggestion would be to make Calvin vice president of the committee and get someone a little more experienced, like Snoopy, to handle the finances. If you need any help getting this off the ground—call me!

Janice McGuire
Salinas

Cat lovers were not always receptive to Ernest's campaigning.

## SOCKS FOR CONGRESS

The full-page ad appearing in the Herald's front section on Jan. 11 endorsing Ernest the dog for the 17th District congressional seat is a cat-darned shame. Albeit, the country is going to the dogs – all the more reason not to put forth any more loud, tail-wagging candidates, but to rally behind independent thinkers who put some thought before their wisely chosen moves.

Meow. I say, Socks for Congress!

Mr. Snugs and Ms. Loki,
Housemates with Bonnie Parker
Salinas

*(Editor's note: Although* The Herald *announced on Sunday that candidate endorsement letters would be printed beginning Feb. 1, we decided that an exception was justified for the above letter on the grounds that Socks, the White House cat, is not an official candidate.)*

Naturally, I took the Editor's note to imply that Ernest *was* an official candidate. Or maybe the Editor just likes cats better than dogs.

The writer of one letter expressed concern about potential Constitutional obstacles to Ernest's candidacy:

## LEGAL HURDLE FOR ERNEST?
Editor, The Herald:

On the face of it, Ernest might be the ideal candidate. (The Herald, Jan. 11.) True, he is probably illiterate, but that has been no bar to many past incumbents or, obviously, to some current ones. However, there is unfortunately a serious legal impediment to his being elected, and I don't mean his caninity.

To quote from Article I, Section 2 of the U.S. Constitution: "No person shall be a Representative who shall not have attained to the age of 25 years, and have been seven years a citizen of the United States, and who shall not, when elected, be an inhabitant of that state in which he shall be chosen."

Note that, although it does say "person," nowhere does the Constitution specifically deny any privilege to anyone or anything on the basis of species. Indeed, there are no doubt any number of legislators ready to debate whether "person" means the same thing as "human being"—if they thought it might be to their advantage somehow to do so.

Ernest may or may not, depending on his age, have been here for seven years, but it's much less than likely that he is 25 or more. Few if any dogs ever make it to that august plateau, dog years notwithstanding.

So, for reasons of constitutionality—plus one more—despite the temptation to do so, I shall not vote for Ernest, though I wish him well in whatever other more legitimate and accessible endeavors he may essay.

Clifford L. Wolf,
Pacific Grove

The dogs who "wrote" letters naturally threw their weight behind their fellow canine. One dog was ready to jump into Ernest's campaign with all four paws:

VOLUNTEER FOR ERNEST
What a revelation—my friend Ernest just disclosed his candidacy for the 17th District U.S. Representative (The Herald, Jan. 11).

I have to agree with him having a long familiarity with this area. I offered my services as an assistant campaign manager.

He naturally wanted to know my qualifications.

I told Ernest that I had my degree of GFD (Good and Faithful Dog) from No Bark University.

We were both in agreement as to political philosophy. The only addition I proposed was a platform of a red fireplug on every corner. The basic platform was honesty, integrity and good sense. Something our Washington politicians are not familiar with.

Our new Canine Coalition is going to prevail and when we are installed will correct all the problems this country is now experiencing.

I am sure that as an intelligent canine with a quality upbringing, I will get along with Ernest and rise to great heights with him.

I will let you know at a later date our progress in the polls.

Keep your paws crossed and we will welcome all contributions to our cause. Just make sure all dog biscuits are fresh and we promise to acknowledge all donations.

Love and licks to our supporters.

Plato, by
Robert C. Cahall,
Carmel

A beagle let us know of her support in her owner's letter:

ROSIE BACKS ERNEST
Our beagle Rosie wishes to announce that she will not be a candidate for the 17th Congressional District. Instead she is throwing her considerable weight behind Ernest (The Herald, Jan. 11).

Because of a philosophical conflict, she will not run for dogcatcher. On the other paw, she is sleeping on the idea of running for mayor, and may soon announce a schedule of neighborhood walks to test the political climate.

An avid C-Span watcher (through her eyelids), Rosie knows that a critter of Ernest's breeding, stature, disposition and Swiss background can convince those elusive "quorums" to come running when he barks, so they can get on with the ayes and nays in the House.

She also thinks the older canines on Capitol Hill (Boxer, Kerry, Hunter, Fox, Gordon and Wolf) need more obedience schooling, and that rowdy litter of yipping GOP puppies needs paper training.

Larry Hawkins
Seaside

A *Carmel Pine Cone* reader wrote this letter to the Editor:

VOTE FOR ERNEST

As I looked deep into Ernest's calm eyes, I realized this was my candidate.

He could not possibly bark one line and vote another. He was too honorable to "streetwalk" with sellout compromises. He is not a member of a one-world government organization.

He is loyal. He is honest. He would die for us without ever asking why.

My perplexity is: What if the electorate chooses him for every possible office up for election?

Ann Dice, Carmel

*Pine Cone* columnist Joe Fitzpatrick delivered his take on Ernest's campaign. Joe writes a really funny column and doesn't hesitate to poke good-natured fun at people and happenings on the Monterey Peninsula.

PUTTING ON THE DOGMA

Well, darned if Pebble Beach's Alan Shugart doesn't think the American system is broken and the problems are far too great to be solved by politicians.

But Al, chairman of Seagate Technology Inc. of Scotts Valley (a world leader in computer disc drives), is a crack problem solver, himself, and he has the answer:

HE's running his DOG for Congress!

He's what? He's running his dog for Congress, and this should solve everything.

So far, Shugart has spent several thousand dollars on newspaper ads announcing his candidacy! Announcing the dog's candidacy, not Al's.

Does this sort of publicity stunt trivialize the whole political process? Does it discourage some highly qualified people from running at all because of the negative connotation it attaches to all people in political office?

Or does it simply indicate Al may have too much free time on his hands?

Carmel Valley's Jill Margaret Brown has no idea about the answers to any of those questions, but she does have strong reservations about the qualifications of the Shugart dog.

"As I understand it," said J.M.B. on the horn, "the pooch is a Bernese Mountain Dog and that should raise all sorts of red flags right there.

"That breed arrived in Switzerland with the ancient Roman soldiers, and do we really want an Italian army groupie in Congress?"

Well, I thought to myself, we've already got Sonny Bono in there, so would this be any...

Before I could finish my thought, J.M.B. was off and running again:

"According to Simon and Schuster's *Guide to Dogs*," she continued, "the Bernese Mountain Dog is 'impetuous...suspicious of strangers...and often unruly.'

"But isn't ONE Bob Dornan enough in Congress?"

I could tell the Shugart dog (named "Ernest") wasn't going to get J.M.B.s vote.

"I've got nothing against dogs," she said, winding down now, "but if we're going to ELECT one, it shouldn't be an immigrant from Berne, Switzerland, whose main qualification is that he's housebroken! In the House we're talking about, that could make him a real outcast!

"Instead, it should be a true-blue, down home, apple pie, darn tootin', all-American dog—like a Great Dane, or a German Shepherd, or a French Poodle, or a Chihuahua, or a Chinese Shar-Pei, or a Scottie!"

Right on!

As for me, I'm still mulling that thing about Shugart's free time.

That same day, *Coast Weekly* carried this item:

ERNEST GOES TO WASHINGTON

Ernest, a three-year-old, 110-pound, Bernese mountain dog, recently announced his candidacy for Congress in the 17th District. Ernest's owner and campaign manager, Al Shugart—who holds a day-job as president of Seagate Technology Inc.—says, "I don't know how to fix the government but the ultimate protest [to how things are being run now] would be to elect a dog."

Ernest, a member of No Political Party (NPP), began his campaign over three months ago, and although he has gained some support (a man from Massachusetts sent $1,000, and another from San Jose sent $500), he still has some hoops to jump through.

Shugart says Ernest can't get a social security number, which keeps him from registering to vote.

But that may be the least of the would-be contender's problems. According to Monterey County Registrar Tony Anchundo, the dog isn't qualified for candidacy because he's not a U.S. citizen. "Someone can go ahead and write the dog's name in," Anchundo says, "but if he's not an official write-in, we don't have to tabulate the votes."

The write-in issue was a problem. We still hadn't figured out how to become "official" so that Ernest's votes could be tabulated.

A feline named Peaches N. Cream, displayed her loyalty in writing: "I'm all for sending Ernest to Washington. Please accept this contribution from my people-bank...I am appalled at what the two-legged creatures have created there. While you're at it, "Socks" needs to be run out of the White House..."

And that from a cat!

A handsome canine named "Lucky" sent a photo of himself lying on the hearth before a fire. He wrote, regarding his political views,

"As you can see in my photo we take the same position." Lucky was right; Ernest's favorite position is lying down.

A cat named "Smokey," while not thrilled with the idea of a dog running for political office, wrote, "a *dog* is at least a step in the right direction." Smokey's owner, Mrs. Lenox, however, considers herself a Friend of Ernest.

Nancy Lenox wrote "to express my support for Ernest's campaign for Congress. If the country is going to the dogs, I couldn't imagine a more qualified canine to lead the way. I believe the late Bosco, former mayor of Sunol, is to date the only elected canine official in the State of California, and it's about time someone followed in his pawprints." Nancy concluded, "it seems like the sharks and the porkers have a good deal more representation than the canines these days."

Two letters we received were from professional people. It seemed Ernest's candidacy was being taken seriously. One letter was from a consultant who addressed his letter to Ernest, included his credentials, and offered the services of his consulting firm.

Another consultant and Appraiser, LeRoy H. Carroll, also wrote to Ernest on a business letterhead:

*This is just a short note to let you know, that unless our country returns to the set of values expressed in your wonderful ad, we won't have even a dog's life. So I commend your friends for their sense of humor, and the willingness to spend some money upon what many of my friends would say is "silliness." For the 535 people we have elected, turn into crooks and liars (the majority), the President is a total disgrace, and the Supreme Court makes laws which Constitutionally they have no right to make. This kennel we call the U.S. of A. is in serious trouble. But with friends, such as yours, we can in turn make a big difference. Please keep on…keeping on.*

Roland Shaw, 3,000 miles away in Florida, had this to say to Ernest:

*I'll be dog gone; finally the people of California have the opportunity to make a choice. I have no bone to pick with another dog running for Congress and enclosed is a small contribution to help in your campaign to represent us, the underdogs. I don't know whether to admire your fortitude, or question your instincts in leaping into this "dog eat dog" business, but it is exciting to think a pure breed could teach the old dogs, mutts and curs some new tricks and wean this country off the gravy train.*

Not all the letters were supportive of Ernest's candidacy. One writer was critical of my spending a significant amount of money on "inane" campaign ads, complaining about a government under which I have succeeded financially, rather than going out into the streets to find people who need real help to get out of their miseries.

A couple of people wrote to express their frustrations regarding their dealings with specific local elected officials, with the expectation of Ernest who they thought might do something to remedy their situation.

Michael DeLapa, a local environmental and business consultant, penned this thoughtful and compelling letter:

*Dear Ernest and Owner of Ernest:*

*Without a doubt, politics in America is cause for despair and cynicism. Like you, I have grown distressed with state and national politics. The trivial and the critical seem hopelessly intermixed, and our government representatives seem incapable of providing meaningful leadership on either. No wonder you have chosen to run a campaign based on the premise that our country is "going to the dogs"—from all appearances, it is!*

*And still, as I write this, one of the very few letters that I have made time for in weeks, I ask you to reconsider. If you, the companion of one of the most successful and innovative leaders in high technology, can't offer guidance in solving some of the important issues that face our country, what hope does that provide the rest of us in your community?*

*Will the humor of your campaign improve or impair public perceptions of government? Will it encourage the public involvement that is so critical in repairing the current system, or will it reinforce the cynicism that is becoming embedded in our society? Should you spend your valuable time, creative talent and tens of thousands of dollars to promote the political tragicomedy, or might you contribute in a more constructive fashion?*

*I hope you will think carefully about your choices as a candidate (and a candidate's owner) and the ways in which your campaign can make a real difference in our lives. I would be pleased to share my ideas about how you can improve the quality of political debate, in particular by becoming involved in campaigns currently underway in Monterey County.*

*Here's hoping that I'm not,
Barking up the wrong tree,*

*Michael D. DeLapa*

One writer found particular pleasure upon reading the full-page ad:

*I want you to know what a big laugh I got when I found Ernest (and Calvin) on page 5A of my* Herald *this morning. I've had an extraordinary amount of stress in my life lately, and your ad is just what I needed, to help me keep things in perspective. My favorite line in the ad is "not a lawyer." (I've been paying plenty of money to lawyers while trying to solve my problems.)*

Like many of the letters that included suggestions to further Ernest's candidacy, this one (written by a beautiful husky who included her photograph), advised that Ernest first run for President in 1996. By the time elected officials reach the Senate, the husky wrote, "'THE SYSTEM' itself has corrupted them irrevocably," so Ernest would more effectively serve the country by using the "Bully Pulpit" of the presidency.

People of all ages were expressing their support of Ernest's candidacy. One fifteen-year-old sent Ernest a note of encouragement and an 84-year-old widow in a Senior Care Center wrote that she was "scared for our country."

My granddaughter Janette distributed bumper stickers and buttons at her elementary school. She said that kids were threatening to misbehave unless the adults agreed to "vote for the dog."

•

The letters continued.

Mel Vercoe, a prolific writer of letters to the *Herald* editor expressed his enjoyment of Ernest's full-page advertisement:

*Your ad in this morning's* Herald *really made my day. I hope it catches on nationally, like in the Doonsbury strip. Seriously, it does appear that we are in danger of losing our*

*country (in my opinion). Nothing else seems to work, as a means of getting people to notice some serious problems.*

Gary Koeppel, owner of Coast Galleries, wrote to Treasurer Calvin and expressed his generous endorsement of Ernest:

*Sending Ernest to Washington is one howl of an idea! He's right. Washington has gone to the politicians, who have gone too farr, and it needs to go to the dogs — but the right dogs. Only a hound can command the candor and caninity to sniff out and dig up the now-buried treasures of America: self regulation, self reliance and self restraint. Enclosed is my check for 25 bones.*

His generous "bones" were the kind Calvin could take to the bank—a check for twenty-five dollars.

We decided to reprint the full-page Ernest ad as a campaign poster. It was red, white, blue—and big.

Pierre and Marietta Bain, my friends and partners in Fandango, a popular Pacific Grove restaurant, displayed the Ernest campaign poster on the wall of their main dining room. We had to give them a second one, because the chefs in the kitchen wanted one there too. The poster was a great conversation piece. It was placed in the window of a number of stores around town, too. I heard the posters were good for some local shops. When passers-by walked in to ask about Ernest, they ended up buying something.

The company that printed the posters

asked permission to print extra ones so they could have some to hang up and distribute. They printed about one-hundred extra and didn't charge us for it. The head of the printing company said he wanted the additional press run to be his "campaign contribution."

There were a few Friends of Ernest "outposts" around the country and beyond the American continent. After returning from a Seagate trip in Asia, I was in Honolulu for a brief layover. I was having a casual conversation with Michelle Takemoto, the station manager for Air Service Hawaii. I happened to mention Ernest. She laughed and thought the whole thing was great. We later sent her buttons and bumper stickers, and she became our Friends of Ernest "Hawaii outpost representative."

Another group of Ernest supporters grew spontaneously out of the full-page ad that Monterey County resident Betty Ranallo sent to "Chickie" Marrington in Gold Hill, Oregon. Chickie and a number of Gold Hill locals walk into town every morning for coffee and donuts. "The coffee shop is our social club," Chickie wrote. "I show Ernest's advertisement to everyone who comes in. We have more fun with it!"

One "Breakfast Club" regular Marilyn Ellertsen offered her services as "Campaign Manager for the Pacific Northwest Region." She wrote, "I envisioned my headquarters for Ernest located in Ray's grocery, so I could hit the maximum number of people in our area. I was really psyched up."

It didn't seem to matter to Gold Hill residents that only voters in California's 17th District could vote for Ernest; he was their candidate.

Responses to the ad and articles about Ernest were overwhelmingly positive and supportive. People wanted to be involved, be part of the action. The concept of Ernest's candidacy had touched a nerve among people of all ages and all walks of life.

In spite of all the fun we were having, I wanted Ernest's campaign to have a relevant political aspect. With the budget debacle clouding the work on Capitol Hill and stimulating negative editorial commentary in the newspapers, Friends of Ernest released to the media Ernest's statements about the current failure to solve the budgetary crisis. On January 19, 1996, Ernest called for a swift resolution of the futile debate, and urged voters to make a wise choice in the November elections.

# Friends of Ernest

## PRESS RELEASE

CANDIDATE ERNEST CALLS FOR BALANCED BUDGET RIGHT NOW

*Time To Stop Pussy-Footing Around, Says Congressional Hopeful*

CARMEL, Calif. — January 19, 1996 — As President Clinton and Republican leaders continue to grapple over whose detailed, government-certified plan will best balance the federal budget in seven years, independent congressional candidate, Ernest, called for an immediate end to the pussy-footing by balancing the budget now.

"Neither side has any earthly idea whether its plan will really balance the federal budget in seven years," Ernest conveyed to his loyal supporters. "If this were a business, you can be sure shareholders would never tolerate another seven years of operating in the red."

Both Republicans and Democrats have based their calculations on assumptions and have stretched numbers so far in seeking a compromise that something was sure to go wrong, conveyed Ernest. He emphasized this point following statements made last week from Stanley Collender, the director of federal budget policy for the accounting firm Price Waterhouse, who said that regardless of the plan Republicans and Democrats come up with, the best America will see by 2002 is a deficit of about $100 billion a year.

"Enough is enough. Put an end to the maneuvering and political jockeying," barked Ernest. "Just do your job, Congress and Mr. President, and balance the budget now."

Promising bold new leadership and a commitment to common sense in government, Ernest earlier this month announced his candidacy to represent California's 17th District in the U.S. Congress.

"I have little confidence in the government to ever really balance the budget — or do anything else of much value, for that matter," said Al Shugart, chairman of Seagate Technology, Inc., and the congressional candidate's chairman. "It's time to rid Congress of Democrats and Republicans alike. It is time for common sense to reign again. If you agree, you'll vote for Ernest."

# 5 February 16, 1996

## Official Recognition

**L**ate in January we finally received the Federal Election Commission information packet and forms we had requested in September. We filled out and returned the forms required, listing "Friends of Ernest" as the Campaign Committee. We then filled in "Ernest" as the Candidate, "Calvin" as Treasurer, and my Assistant, Karen Seifert, as Deputy Chairman and Assistant Treasurer. Calvin signed with an "X," and I signed right after his "X" as Campaign Chairman. We sent off the paperwork on February 9.

I wasn't sure how the FEC would react to the Friends of Ernest campaign committee application. I thought the odds of their accepting Ernest's candidacy were slim. But the public's response to Ernest was encouraging, so while waiting for the FEC response, we moved forward with the campaign.

On February 7 Robin Musitelli of *The Santa Cruz County Sentinel* asked local political candidates to fill out a profile questionnaire. Ernest was included in the mailing. Robin encouraged those completing the questionnaire: "Have fun. Be thoughtful. Be brief." We could do that.

Meanwhile, the electioneering, the caucuses and the New Hampshire primary were in full swing. Friends of Ernest wanted to be sure the public knew that canine candidate Ernest would not engage in negative campaigning. In our press release of February 12, 1996, Ernest promised to set a good example throughout the campaign.

---

| I certify that I have examined this Statement and to the best of my knowledge and belief it is true, correct and complete. | | |
|---|---|---|
| TYPE OR PRINT NAME OF TREASURER <br><br> CALVIN | SIGNATURE OF TREASURER <br> X Calvin    By: *Alan F. Shugar* <br> Campaign Chairman | DATE <br><br> February 9, 1996 |
| NOTE: Submission of false, erroneous, or incomplete information may subject the person signing this Statement to the penalties of 2 U.S.C. §437g. <br> ANY CHANGE IN INFORMATION SHOULD BE REPORTED WITHIN 10 DAYS. | | |

| | | | | For further information contact: <br> Federal Election Commission <br> Toll-free 800-424-9530 <br> Local 202-219-3420 | FE5AN045 | **FEC FORM 1** <br> (revised 4/87) |
|---|---|---|---|---|---|---|

*Santa Cruz* **Sentinel** *County*

207 Church Street, P.O. Box 638
Santa Cruz, California 95061 / 408-423-4242
Fax No. 408-423-1154

PROFILE

|  |  |
|---|---|
| Name: | ERNEST |
| Age: | 3 years |
| Occupation: | Security Guard and Companion |
| Where I live and family: | I live in Pebble Beach with friends, but have lost touch with my family. I believe my mother and father still live in Redding, California, where I was born. |
| Most recent personal accomplishment: | My most recent <u>canine</u> accomplishment was listening to the reading of the complete U.S. Constitution, all amendments, and the Declaration of Independence, all without a break. |
| What people don't know about me: | There is <u>nothing</u> hidden about me. |
| First hero and why: | Calvin was my first hero, because he knew all about the place where we live when I arrived. He shared his knowledge with me. |
| Current hero and why: | My Campaign Chairman, Al Shugart, is my current hero. Al believes I can do more with my life, and the food has gotten better since I became a candidate. |
| Last book I read: | Unfortunately, I am unable to read. |
| Pet peeve: | My pet peeve is the use of some derogatory canine expressions like, "until the last dog is hung." |
| Personal quote: | I tell my friends at the SPCA: "You, too, can better yourself, if you can just get out of here." |

**FEDERAL ELECTION COMMISSION**
999 E Street, N.W.
Washington, D.C. 20463

**ACKNOWLEDGEMENT OF RECEIPT**
**OF**
Statement of Organization

Filed pursuant to the Federal Election Campaign Act of 1971, as amended

CALVIN, Treasurer
FRIENDS OF ERNEST
P O BOX 5908
CARMEL           CA  93921

DATE: 02/16/1996

**NOTICE REGARDING FILINGS**
**UNDER THE FEDERAL ELECTION CAMPAIGN ACT OF 1971, AS AMENDED**
C00313130

Your assigned FEC IDENTIFICATION NUMBER is

In the future this number should be entered on all subsequent reports filed under the Act, as well as on all communications concerning such reports and statements. This acknowledgement will be the only receipt provided directly by the Commission, for documents filed. The Commission recommends that all future filings be mailed Certified or Registered, Return Receipt Requested, in order to insure timeliness of your filings and to provide additional receipts for your records.

**FEDERAL ELECTION COMMISSION**

**FEC FORM 20 (9/87)**
(Supersedes FEC Forms 13, 14, and 15)

---

The Federal Election Commission replied two weeks after we sent our application forms. The FEC acknowledged Friends of Ernest as "an authorized committee of a candidate for federal office" and assigned FOE an official ID number. (Ernest was also assigned a candidate ID number.)

When I showed the correspondence to Karen, who had filled out the application forms with me, she could hardly believe it. I was surprised, too.

We were official!

I had barely gotten over the good news when I noticed an amusing item in the FEC campaign regulations. Calvin, as Treasurer, would bear the liability if a violation of law occurred. I thought that was funny. If we broke the law not only would poor old Calvin be in the doghouse, he'd be heading for jail!

●

Our biggest boost to date had derived from the full-page ad. Most thought it was great. Some considered it outrageous. It was intended above all as a protest, and the large majority recognized it as such and enjoyed the humor. Their response egged us on and kept us going. The flood of letters and support coming in from all over the world encouraged us even more. So many people were behind our effort. We started seeing bumper stickers all around Santa Cruz and Monterey counties.

Still, if the FEC hadn't accepted our submissions and given us an official organization number, the campaign might have ended right there. But the acceptance and all the subsequent letters and regular reports they sent spurred us on.

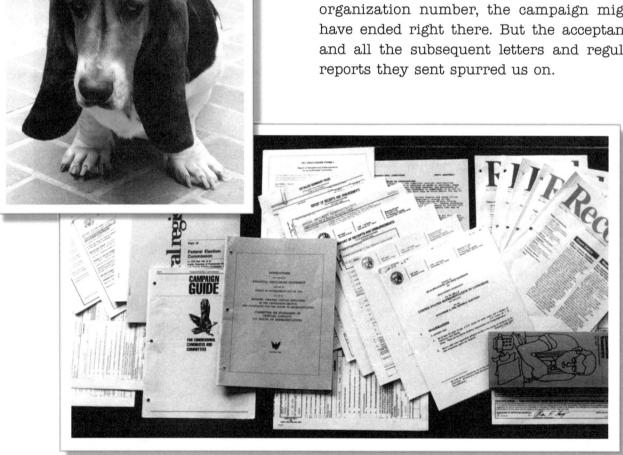

## FEDERAL ELECTION COMMISSION
WASHINGTON, D.C. 20463

C00313130
FRIENDS OF ERNEST
CALVIN
P O BOX 5908
CARMEL, CA 93921

02/19/1996

Dear Treasurer:

Our records show that you have registered an authorized committee of a candidate for federal office. To help your committee understand the election law, we have enclosed several publications (see attachment).

We offer this assistance to help you avoid any violation of the federal election law (U.S.C. Title 2) or the regulations prescribed by the Federal Election Commission (11 CFR). As treasurer, you are responsible for your committee's compliance with the election law. (See, for example, 2 U.S.C. sections 432(c), (d) and (i) and 11 CFR 102.7(c), 103.3(a) and 104.14(d).) This means that in the event that the Commission brings an enforcement action against your committee, absent unusual circumstances, you will be named as a respondent along with the committee. Moreover, you may be held personally liable if a violation of law occurs and the committee is unable to pay the required penalty.

To further assist you, we have added your name to our mailing list for our monthly publication, the RECORD. If you wish to order additional free subscriptions for other members of your staff, please give us a call (see below).

If you have any questions about your role, the law or the publications, please contact the Information Division at 1/800-424-9530 or 202/219-3420.

Attachments
 – 'Committee Treasurer' brochure (see especially p. 4)
 – Federal Election Campaign Act (2 U.S.C. Titles 2 & 26)
 – FEC Regulations (11 CFR)
 – FEC Form 1: Statement of Organization
 – FEC Form 3 (with supporting schedules)
 – List of State Filing Offices
 – Schedule of Reporting Dates
 – Copy of the RECORD, the FEC monthly newsletter

Bobby Werfel, Deputy
Assistant Staff Director
Information Division

*Celebrating the Commission's 20th Anniversary*
YESTERDAY, TODAY AND TOMORROW
DEDICATED TO KEEPING THE PUBLIC INFORMED

•

Several more letters of support arrived in February. "Here's an idea absolutely free," Catherine Borka wrote. "Instead of buttons and bumper stickers (which the other guys use) give out pooper-scoopers! Establish Ernest as an environmentalist!"

This *was* a great idea, but Calvin was keeping a short leash on campaign funds. Buttons and bumper stickers would have to suffice.

The four-footed "Citizens for an Ernest Voice" sent us their message with their handsome canine photos. "Toby," "Logan," and "Max" wrote: "We, the undersigned, do hereby support a good friend and great creature. We all deserve an Ernest voice in Washington. Let's put some bite back into the bark."

Another letter arrived for Ernest from "many enthusiastic supporters in the Greater Metropolitan Los Angeles Area. One of the fans told Ernest: "Yesterday a man in San Dimas, on hearing of your strong assets, declared, 'And he's *not an incumbent!* That's the best point of all.'"

•

The Santa Cruz campus of the University of California publishes a campus newspaper called *The Fish Rap Live!* Staff writer Andria Strickley came to my Scotts Valley office and interviewed me for the February 14, 1996 issue. "No More Chasing Balls; Lift Your Leg On Congress" was the caption of her front page feature. The following are some of the highlights:

Shugart says that he made the decision to have Ernest run out of his own frustration with the political system, describing it as "broken." He says that he sees the campaign as a platform for people (and dogs) from all walks of life to voice dissent.

"All the Senate rules and House rules have to be disbanded. These rules are voluminous, and they're inhibiting. The whole system has to be scrapped so we can start all over again," says Shugart. "Now, I'm not the only person who thinks that way, but I'm the only one who had a dog named Ernest."

And what does Ernest himself hope to accomplish through his campaign? "He doesn't like to get caught up in issues," says Shugart, "but instead runs on a platform of simple common sense."

Shugart adds that he and Ernest both agree things would run more smoothly in Washington if politicians just followed the Constitution.

"Ernest thinks the Constitution's basically a good document, with all the right intent," says Shugart. "They should have addressed the dog issue probably, though. Nobody had it in their wildest dreams when they wrote the Constitution that some crazy guy would be running a dog for Congress."

So how would Ernest the dog fare in the rough waters of Washington political life?

"He doesn't understand that it's a full-time job," says Shugart. "He thinks the House ought to meet for a week, maybe every six weeks or so. He still thinks it's a part time job." Shugart says Ernest also believes most politicians spend too much of their time in office trying to get reelected,

# Friends of Ernest

## PRESS RELEASE

### ERNEST CALLS FOR END TO POLITICAL DOG FIGHTING

CARMEL, Calif. — February 12, 1996 — Ernest, an announced candidate for the U.S. House of Representatives from California's 17th District, has called for all candidates for public office to pledge "no negative campaigning."

"It's a sort of a 'contract with the voters,' conveyed Ernest, at a rally held in Pebble Beach during the AT&T Pro-Am golf tournament. "If the behavior shown by the Presidential Candidates in the Iowa caucus and the New Hampshire primary is any indication, this year's presidential election is going to the dogs, and it's up to a canine to set the example. Voters deserve better from their candidates."

Ernest, a member of No Political Party (NPP), has himself been collared by a muckraking Democratic Party Chairman who said he hoped Ernest was "not just another corporate lap dog." Ernest's response makes it clear that this kind of name calling is inappropriate for any dog and pony show.

and he definitely favors term limits.

"He'd probably get so disgusted after a term that he'd want to quit anyway," Shugart says.

Shugart isn't sure what the end result of the campaign will be, but he hopes the statement it's making will be a sounding board for political reform.

"I don't know the answer to this whole thing," Shugart says. "But I thought if I could get enough people in the country concerned about [the political system], maybe someone could come up with the answer."

For now, Ernest will continue to stand by the values he's always held: honesty, ethics, and common sense. If you think about it, you couldn't ask much more from a dog—or a representative.

March 1996 brought Ernest more letters from his supporters, including one from Kathleen Hurley of the American Electronics Association. She sent Ernest some snacks, and a dog bed topped off with colorful balloons. Ernest wrote his own paw-signed thank-you note to Kathleen:

*Thank you so much for the "campaign trail survival kit." Calvin and I ate all the dog biscuits Friday night when Al brought the gift home, and we now have the three very patriotic balloons flying from our dog house. I gave the bed to one of my smaller supporters who lives here.*

*Once again thanks for thinking of me.*

Abe Still—the campaign manager for his daughter's Rottweiler, Graffin, a presidential candidate—sent Calvin copies of his twenty-nine letters to the Editor of *The Union Democrat* of Sonora, California. Abe was generous in sharing his views about the political scene. Graffin, he wrote, "hopes that Ernest can use the material in his campaign for the 17th Congressional District."

Although serious in intent, Abe's letters exhibited laugh-out-loud humor, and offered some well-conceived ideas for political debate. Graffin was running a "strictly issue-oriented" campaign, Abe told me. In his letters, Abe tackled taxation, abortion, separation of church and state, gun control, campaign finance reform, minority rights, welfare reform, foreign policy. I had a good time reading Abe's letters and appreciated Abe's—and Graffin's—views on what's ailing in Washington.

By now, the campaign trail was proving to be a bumpy ride. Ernest still hadn't succeeded in getting a Social Security number, and without that he couldn't be a registered voter and couldn't get on the ballot either in Santa Cruz or Monterey County. We had tried every avenue, but without success. In another attempt to get a number issued, I wrote to the Commissioner of the Internal Revenue Service on March 15, 1996.

The delays and dead ends on Ernest's road to a place on the ballot would not put an end to the campaign. It was alive and well, and the media helped to keep it in the public eye. And attention continued to come from the other side of the Atlantic. I received a faxed copy of an article published in *The UK Microscope* on January 31, 1996. In it, reporter Erin English quotes Monterey

# Friends of Ernest

March 15, 1996

Margaret Milner Richardson
Commissioner
Internal Revenue Service
1111 Constitution Avenue, N.W.
Washington, DC 20224

Dear Commissioner Richardson:

My friend Ernest has a problem. He has become a working dog and wants to make certain he follows all the tax laws. He presently is self-employed, but if he is successful in his congressional bid in the 17th District, the United States Government will become his employer.

Even without his election, his income this year may reach the level requiring filing of a tax return. Recognizing the need for a Social Security number, Ernest applied, but was rejected. The Social Security contact suggested to call the Internal Revenue Service about the tax liability. Therefore, this letter.

Please advise.

Yours Sincerely,

Alan F. Shugart

Registrar of Voters Tony Anchundo, who said of Ernest: "I'm sure the dog has his tags and has received all his shots, but that's not enough." Anchundo told English it was the first time in his career that a dog had been presented as a candidate for office, but added that Mickey Mouse had been put forth in the past.

On March 15 Seagate's Paris office faxed me a copy of an article about the company that appeared in the March 14/15 issue of *CeBIT News*, in the official English language edition. (CeBIT is the World Business Center Office for Information and Telecommunications, which holds annual international trade fairs in Hannover, Germany.) CeBIT publishes significant news and reports about business and industry worldwide.

The subject matter of this long and detailed article, entitled "Seagate Acquires, Shines," was about the company's growth. The tone and content was serious, but here's now the article began:

Al Shugart laughed out loud when, starting the interview, I asked how Ernest was.

"Ernest is fine. We are working hard to see that he will get elected," he chuckled. Ernest is one of Shugart's pet dogs running for the Californian Senate. For real. His pal in the political doghouse, his financial controller, has been receiving $1,000 donations, thank you very much. It's a nice way out for the CEO of a $4.5 billion company to see eye-to-eye with the relativity of life.

The March 18 issue of *Business Week* contained a three-page feature about me and Seagate. Writer Peter Burrows couldn't resist referring to Ernest at the outset:

THE MAN IN THE DRIVER'S SEAT

Buying Conner puts Seagate's Al Shugart squarely on top. Talk to Silicon Valley executives, and they'll tell you Seagate Technology CEO Alan F. Shugart is one of a kind—certainly the only one among them running his pet for Congress. "The nation is going to the dogs," Shugart declares, "and I don't know what else to do about it."

He's trying to get Ernest, his Bernese mountain dog, on the ballot to give disgruntled voters a way to vent their feelings. There are Ernest buttons, a campaign committee (FOE, for Friends of Ernest) that has raised $3,000, and press releases—the latest bemoaning the "dogfighting" among Republican candidates. Shugart even hit up suppliers. "I talk to him every few weeks about that damn dog," laughs Adaptec Chairman John G. Adler, who coughed up $500.

Ernest isn't mentioned in the remainder of the article, but the story included a photo of me wearing a white sweat shirt with Ernest's picture on it and the words, "Take a Bite Outta Congress" and Ernest's picture on it.

•

Getting Ernest on the election ballot was always the primary objective of the campaign.

Charlie Robb, of the Florida-based Smith Agency was apparently prepared to do even more than that. He faxed me his letter on March 18. In it he wrote:

*…I am the Creative Director for an advertising firm in Ft. Lauderdale, Florida. And Ernie's campaign is just the kind of pro bone-o account we'd like to sink our teeth into. I would therefore like to offer the services of The Smith Agency to Ernie and FOE.*

*We already have a few ideas that we'd like to run past Ernie. And a number of questions about his positions on various issues. For instance, we're pretty sure he's for quality healthcare…but does that include cat scans?*

*As to handling the press, we have a few suggestions for how Ernie should respond when attacked by the print media. Release photos of Ernie (with the offending edition), reliving the part of his youth when newspapers were a very functional part of his house training.*

*We also think it's important to position Ernie as a watchdog for congressional reform. After all, genetically who is better suited for the job?*

*Basically, we see this campaign as a balancing act. We need to make Ernie appear friendly and approachable, but not to the point of rolling over. It's a challenge. On the one hand, a grass roots campaign. On the other, a candidate that on a bad day might actually eat the grass. We'll have to work on that.*

*Mr. Shugart, we are excited about the prospect of helping Ernie realize his political ambitions. We understand there have been unsubstantiated rumors regarding Ernie's love life. No problem. With the right handlers, we're confident we can keep Ernie out of the dog house long enough to get him elected. With that under his belt, there's no reason why he couldn't go all the way. Top dog.*

*And we're ready to help. The services of our agency are at your command…as long as the command isn't heel or sit or fetch.*

It was a generous offer, but one we had to decline. I thanked Charlie and let him know that getting Ernest on the ballot had to be achieved before trying to get him elected.

When Charlie learned that "Ernie" was not the correct name, he faxed his apology, adding, "I guess you could say it was a faux paw."

During the first few months of 1996 Ernest received so much publicity that whenever and wherever I spoke or was interviewed, Ernest was invariably the first topic addressed. Even at Seagate-related engagements everyone wanted the latest campaign news. The adventures of the candidate did inevitably capture the opening questions and elicited the most laughs. Clearly, the concept had resonated with people.

As I said, enjoyment of the Ernest protest wasn't limited to the United States. Seagate has offices and plants around the world. I hold thirty or forty quarterly meetings with employees, and travel coast to coast in North America, and to Europe and Asia every three months. The campaign, long since over, continues to be a frequent topic. Employees still ask about Ernest: What's he doing now? Will he'll run again?

We're still having fun with it!

☆ ☆ ☆ ☆ ☆ ☆ ☆ ☆ ☆ ☆ ☆ ☆ ☆

# 6

# March 26, 1996

# Primary Underdog, Independent Topdog

At lunchtime on March 26, the day of California's primary election, Pierre and Marietta—my partners in the Pacific Grove restaurant Fandango—were surprised to see two large Bernese Mountain Dogs show up at the door. Each of the dogs had an owner in tow.

"Is this the polling place?" one of the owners—a frequent patron—asked.

The Bains were understandably puzzled.

The other owner explained that they'd seen the campaign ad posted at Fandango earlier in the year.

"We figured if a Bernese Mountain Dog could run for Congress, our two dogs could vote for him!"

It was a good chuckle for the Bains—and the lunch customers who overheard the exchange—but they had to report that Ernest hadn't qualified for the ballot.

With much tail wagging and head shaking, the dogs and their owners conveyed their condolences and departed.

•

After the primary election, Friends of Ernest wanted to assure supporters and the media that although Ernest's name did not appear on the primary ballot—since he wasn't party-affiliated—he was still very active as an independent candidate.

On April 1, a FOE campaign worker called the Monterey County Elections Office to inquire about the number of write-in votes for Ernest. A spokesperson there told FOE that although the Elections Office had not yet finalized its official tally of the March 26 votes, "only votes for 'qualified' candidates would be counted. Ernest is not a qualified candidate." The Santa Cruz Elections Office issued a similar statement.

This refusal to acknowledge Ernest's votes didn't deter his committed friends. Letters of support boosted the briefly sagging spirits of Ernest and Calvin. Their loyal canine contingent continued to put paw and pen to paper and pledge support for their candidate.

"Possaroo" wrote and offered himself as running mate. Described as 3/4 whippet and 1/4 white German shepherd, and resembling a deer, this canine had definite potential.

# Friends of Ernest

## PRESS RELEASE

### ERNEST CALLS FOR MORE VOTER PARTICIPATION
*Underdog Steps Up Campaign Effort*

SANTA CRUZ, Calif. — March 27, 1996 — Ernest, an announced candidate for Congress from California's 17th District, conveyed to a rally in downtown Santa Cruz the day following the California Primary that we need more voters if we are to eliminate the packs of politicians running our country.

Ernest, who did not participate in the partisan primary due to his non-affiliation with any political party, communicated that "District 17 voters have selected their top elephant and top donkey, and now it's time to concentrate on the top dog." Ernest is urging all eligible but unregistared voters to register to vote in the November 5th election. Ernest further begged those non-voting registered voters to get involved and support the "common sense" candidate. When asked to speak on the issue of this nation's non-voting armchair politicians, Ernest simply reminded the crowd of Plato's words, "Those who are too smart to engage in politics will be punished by being governed by those who are dumber."

Ernest barked his approval: With his grace and style, Possaroo could outrun any opposing running mate.

A letter of a different sort came from Sharon Parsons, a member of the local PROTECT Committee, who wrote:

*Dear Ernest,*

*Sorry you lost your effort to go to Congress. You are a handsome clever fellow who would have made a national splash.*

*You can still be a hero on the county level and bring some common sense to local government if you are willing to put your leftover campaign funds where your bark is.*

*Urban sprawl threatens to turn Monterey Co. into another "slurb" like Santa Clara or Los Angeles County.*

*Your contribution will support PROTECT, the committee striving to put a managed growth initiative on the November ballot.*

Ms. Parsons concluded her letter with a request for financial help and enclosed a summary of the initiative and additional information. Although FOE was unable to provide any financial assistance, we did send some stickers and buttons, plus our latest press release.

•

The California primary was already over and I hadn't yet received any reply to my March 15 letter to the IRS. I still wasn't clear on Ernest's tax liability. Did he owe the IRS any money?

By the time I sent them another letter, they finally replied. On April 24, Cheryl Kordick of the IRS informed me that the owner of any animal carried all tax payment responsibilities.

I wasn't satisfied with that response. In everything I write or say about Ernest, I never refer to him as "my dog," or to myself as "his owner." (The one exception was listing myself as "owner" in the original Social Security application—which I regret now.) Ernest is his own dog, and I've always described him as such. I usually call him, "my friend."

I thought about filing an income tax return for Ernest, anyway, but I was doing a lot of travel for Seagate at the time. I never got around to it.

Eventually, I did get around to responding to Cheryl Kordick at the IRS. I implied that Ernest couldn't be owned because of Constitutional Amendment XIII which prohibits slavery. The IRS never replied. And it doesn't appear that the Supreme Court was ever given a chance to consider the issue.

•

I am an avid reader and I keep informed about world events, national and local news. While reading the *San Francisco Chronicle*, I came across a letter to the Editor asking, "Where's the Good News?" The writer asked for more media coverage of the good things that were happening. She concluded, "We need hope and inspiration."

I wrote a response in my April 30 letter to the *Chronicle* Editor:

DEPARTMENT OF THE TREASURY
INTERNAL REVENUE SERVICE
WASHINGTON, D.C. 20224

APR 24 1996

Mr. Alan F. Shugart
Friends of Ernest
P. O. Box 5908
Carmel, CA  93921

Dear Mr. Shugart:

This is in response to your March 15, 1996, letter for your friend Ernest concerning his potential tax liability.

Generally, any income earned for the performance of an animal in a trade or business is taxable to the owner.

I hope this information will be helpful to you.

Sincerely,

for Cheryl Kordick, Chief
Assistance Section
Customer Services Branch

*Dear Editor,*

*In her April 27 letter to the Editor, Emily Shihadeh makes a good point about excessive media coverage of bad news. However, I don't think we can blame it all on the media. Contrary to her belief, there isn't a whole lot of good news to report!*

*We talk about the loss of family values but this is just a result of the more general loss of "people" values. We don't trust each other any more; just the effort to get through each day is becoming really complicated and stressful; and last but not least, we have lost our sense of humor.*

*My friend Ernest and I have had long talks on this matter, and he has concluded that broken government systems and the broken political system are the culprits and, of course, whatever led to the breakage. Ernest believes the first step is to throw out all the politicians by electing truly independent candidates. He thinks that unencumbered representation can sort out the problems and fix them.*

*In case you haven't heard, Ernest, a Bernese Mountain Dog, is an announced candidate for Congress from the 17th District, and a member of No Political Party (NPP).*

Seven thousand miles away, Europeans continued to follow Ernest's campaign. The Seagate London office faxed me a note and this brief article from the April 29 *London Daily Telegraph*. It read:

GOING TO THE DOGS

They are just as disillusioned with politics on the other side of the pond. Al Shergar [sic], president of electronics company Seagate, has entered his dog Ernest as a candidate in the Californian congressional elections in November.

His dislike of politicians is shared by his rivals. Dick Egan, chairman of Seagate's competitor EMC, is so taken with the idea he has donated $1,000 to the canine's fighting fund. Why stop at Congress? "Ernest has not reached the minimum age of 35," says EMC spokesman Mike Hardwige. "Even in dog years."

My Seagate colleague added this commentary: "Well, at least they spelled Ernest's name right..." This was not the first time "Shugart" was misspelled on both sides of the Atlantic—and the Pacific!

●

Although Ernest was officially considered a candidate by the Federal Election Commission, he was still not officially on the ballot. On May first a Friends of Ernest campaign worker wrote to Tony Anchundo, Monterey County Registrar of Voters, to find out how to get Ernest on the ballot as a qualified write-in candidate. Anchundo's May 2 reply told the story: Ernest was not a registered voter in Monterey County; without a Social Security number he couldn't register to vote; and he was not of legal voting age.

Well, Ernest did have a few strikes against him But he wasn't out yet. Ernest was still a player in this political ballpark. And the season wasn't over.

Tackling the issue of tort reform, Ernest made his way into the May 3, 1996, issue of *Investors Business Daily*. Brian Deagon, in his "Leaders and Success" byline, wrote a lengthy feature profiling me, Seagate—and Ernest.

"Al Shugart," Deagon began, "is so disgusted with politicians and lawyers that he's sicking his dog on them." He quotes me: "This is my way of protesting how politicians and lawyers have screwed up our government, which is stifling productivity, economic growth and employment...I'm bothered by failure, so I try to do something like running Ernest for Congress."

The article was long and mostly about Seagate and me as the company's CEO. But it was worth noting because once again, Ernest dominates the lead paragraph!

During the week following the publication of this feature, a few letters of encouragement came my way from people in the business community who had read Deagon's article and references to Ernest. "Keep up the good work! I wish I could vote for him!" wrote one Dayton, Ohio, company Vice President.

Ernest continued to gain recognition as a symbol of voter protest. On May 7 a Santa Cruz resident wrote me that he "was going through a very tough experience" doing legal battle with Santa Cruz officials. "I very much appreciate your expression of protest in relation to your Ernest for Congress activities. Please let me know how I can help, I very much would like to. Ernest has my vote."

An editorial in *The Monterey County Herald* prompted me to write to the Editor who published my letter in the Sunday, May 19, edition:

### ERNEST AGREES

I read your May 12 editorial, "Those bedsheet ballots," to my friend Ernest (he can't read), and Ernest could not agree more. However, he doesn't believe the problem is solvable without major surgery to all our government systems. After we take back control of our lives from the federal government, we must seriously reform our state and local systems. Ernest has suggested throwing out all the Republicans and Democrats, and electing true Independent representation. Sounds like it's worth a try.

Alan F. Shugart
Carmel

*(Editor's note: Shugart is campaign manager for Ernest, canine candidate for Congress from the 17th District, and a member of No Political Party.)*

Seagate Corporate Headquarters is located in the Santa Cruz hills and in proximity to the Santa Cruz County SPCA. My family's commitment to help make life better for our four-footed and feathered friends led me to become familiar with the SPCA staff in both Santa Cruz and Monterey Counties, and to help fund their operations.

Having read about criticism leveled against the Santa Cruz SPCA, I sent my comments on the subject to the Editor of the Santa Cruz County Sentinel. My letter was published in the May 15 issue:

# Friends of Ernest

December 11, 1995

Ross Perot
United We Stand America
P.O. Box 516087
Dallas, TX 75251

Dear Ross,

Although you won't be able to vote for Ernest, I thought you might like to see an effort by a few concerned citizens and a really smart dog.

Regards,

Alan F. Shugart

AFS/ko

ERNEST SUPPORTS SPCA

I read Jody Paterniti's SPCA Op-Ed (May 12) to my friend Ernest (Ernest can't read), and he thinks Jody and the Santa Cruz SPCA are getting a bum rap. Ernest has had many friends who have temporarily stayed at the SPCA, and he has never heard any negative comments (with the exception that they were locked up).

Ernest doesn't understand why, with all the major problems we have in the government systems that are controlling our lives, anyone would pick on a well-run SPCA.

Jody Paterniti sent Ernest and me a nice note after reading my letter.

For a brief time, I considered enlisting the support of Ross Perot's Reform Party. I even sent them a letter with some literature. Afterwards I discarded the idea. I didn't want to compromise Ernest's independent position as a non-affiliated candidate. Instead, FOE issued a press release reaffirming Ernest's position as a member of No Political Party. We also stated that we had decided not to accept support from the Reform Party. That turned out to be a moot point. They never asked.

Throughout the campaign, letters and contributions continued to arrive in the mail. One of Ernest's most loyal and generous supporters, Dorothy M. Lund, in her May 23 letter, wrote, "Congratulations on having run a clean primary campaign and on remaining independent. I have your campaign sticker on my car, and frequently wear your button.

I enclose a small donation, perhaps to keep up your strength in the campaign to come."

Ernest wrote and thanked the faithful and generous Charter Member of FOE, and included another button and sticker set. We also sent her a Friends of Ernest Membership Card. (We printed small cards about a month earlier and started sending them to Ernest's supporters to let them know they were Charter Members of FOE.)

●

We were now four months into the campaign and o-o-o-ps! we missed a Federal Election Commission deadline. May 15 slipped by without our filing the candidate's Financial Disclosure Statement. Somehow we'd been moving along with the idea that the financial report was to be filed at the close of the campaign. Not so. We sent in the report on May 24,—nine days late. I don't know whether this delay in filing precipitated extra scrutiny from the Federal Election Commission, but in any event, the result was a flurry of letters from the FEC.

Some of the correspondence was amusing. One letter was addressed to "Mr. Ernest". Another one was addressed to Calvin. Mostly, it seemed like bureaucratic red tape. Nevertheless we did our best to comply with whatever the FEC requested.

While reading a political commentary about campaign finance reform by Philip Chavez, a local Republican congressional candidate, in the June 6, 1996, *Monterey County Herald*, I thought it was important to express my support for reform. I wrote to the *Herald*

FEDERAL ELECTION COMMISSION
WASHINGTON, D.C. 20463

Mr. Ernest                                           MS-H
P.O. Box 1067
Pebble Beach, CA   93953

Candidate ID Number:   H6CA17117          JUN   4 1996

Dear Sir:

This letter constitutes formal written notification that Friends of Ernest has filed reports of receipts and disbursements with the Commission and appears to have received contributions and/or made expenditures in support of your 1996 candidacy in excess of $5,000.   Commission Regulations define a "candidate" as "...an individual who seeks nomination for election, or election, to Federal office, whenever any of the following events occur:

(1) The individual has received contributions aggregating in excess of $5,000 or has made expenditures aggregating in excess of $5,000.

(2) The individual has given his or her consent to another person to receive contributions or make expenditures on behalf of that individual and such person has received contributions aggregating in excess of $5,000 or made expenditures aggregating in excess of $5,000.

(3) After written notification by the Commission that any other person has received contributions aggregating in excess of $5,000 or made expenditures aggregating in excess of $5,000 on the individual's behalf, the individual fails to disavow such activity by letter to the Commission within 30 days receipt of the notification."        (11 CFR $100.3(a))

You have thirty days from receipt of this notification to disavow these activities.   To disavow send a letter directly to the Commission at the above address, marked Attention: Reports Analysis Division, stating that you are not a candidate for

<u>Federal Office and that you have not authorized the solicitation</u>
<u>of contributions nor the making of expenditures on your behalf.</u>

If you do not disavow these activities, you should file a
statement of candidacy (FEC FORM 2). (11 CFR §101.1(a))

If you have any further questions, please contact our Reports
Analysis Division on the toll-free number (800) 424-9530. Our
local number is (202) 219-3580.

Sincerely,

Peter Kell Jr.
Chief, Authorized Branch
Reports Analysis Division

# Friends of Ernest

June 17, 1996

Peter Kell, Jr.
Chief, Authorized Branch
Reports Analysis Division
Federal Election Commission
Washington, DC 20463

Dear Mr. Kell,

I am writing this letter for Ernest who cannot write.

For your convenience I have enclosed a copy of the letter you sent to Ernest dated June 4, 1996. Ernest wishes to advise you that he is indeed a candidate, having submitted a Form 2 as required on February 9, 1996.

Ernest is confused as to how he has a Candidate ID Number, and yet you ask for the filing of a Form 2. Does this mean he has to file another Form 2, or did you just make a mistake?

Ernest would also like to be informed if some outside agency, organization, or person requested that the enclosed letter be sent.

Sincerely,



Alan F. Shugart
Friend of Ernest

cc: Ernest

**FEDERAL ELECTION COMMISSION**
WASHINGTON, D.C. 20463

JUN 4 1996

Calvin
Friends of Ernest
P.O. Box 5908
Carmel, CA 93921

Identification Number: C00313130

Reference: Statement of Organization dated 2/9/96

Dear Treasurer:

This letter is prompted by the Commission's preliminary review of your Statement of Organization. The review raised questions concerning certain information contained in the Statement. An itemization follows:

-Your Statement of Organization (FEC FORM 1) fails to include the signature of the designated Treasurer. Additionally, the full name of the candidate is required for this form to be considered complete. These deficiencies should be corrected and an amended Statement of Organization filed. Please note that the submission of false, erroneous, or incomplete information may subject the person signing this Statement to the penalties of 2 U.S.C. at 437(g).

A written response or an amendment to your original report(s) correcting the above problem(s) should be filed with the Federal Election Commission within fifteen (15) days of the date of this letter. If you need assistance, please feel free to contact me on our toll-free number, (800) 424-9530. My local number is (202) 219-3580.

Sincerely,

Ginger Campbell
Reports Analyst
Reports Analysis Division

# Friends of Ernest

June 24, 1996

Ginger Campbell
Reports Analyst
Reports Analysis Division
Federal Election Commission
Washington, DC 20463

**Re: Your letter to "Treasurer" of June 4, 1996 (enclosed for your convenience)**

Dear Ms. Campbell,

We don't believe that an amendment to our FEC Form 1 submitted on February 9, 1996, is needed.

First of all, Calvin, Treasurer of Friends of Ernest, cannot write. I therefore signed the Form 1, following the printed name of the Treasurer. Calvin accepted this as perfectly proper, and has accepted the responsibilities of office.

Secondly, the candidate's complete name is Ernest. While the AKC identified him with a surname at birth, Ernest has never used this surname nor any initials. (His AKC surname is Von Taplacs.) All of the candidate's and campaign committee's collateral, advertising, and press releases, as well as all the media mention, have referred to the candidate as Ernest. To require the Form 1 to be resubmitted with the addition of a surname which has not been used since birth, would be misleading to people searching for filed information about the candidate. Wouldn't you expect to find information about Madonna without knowing her last name (if she has one)?

Of much greater concern to Friends of Ernest is what is a "preliminary review," and why now? It would seem to us that upon receipt of the Form 1 in February and issuance of an FEC number to the committee, that a "preliminary review" had been done. After all, it's only one page.

Please consider this as a formal request for any information the FEC may have, related to any inquiries or requests about Ernest or Friends of Ernest, from any outside people, agencies, or organizations. We frankly are beginning to suspect dirty politics.

Sincerely,


Alan F. Shugart
Campaign Chairman

Friends of Ernest • PO Box 5908 • Carmel • CA 93921 • Treasurer: Calvin

Editor who published my letter in the June 14 edition:

ERNEST CHAVEZ'S FRIEND

I read Commentary by Philip Chavez (June 6) to my friend Ernest (he can't read) and he thinks Mr. Chavez makes perfect sense.

I listened to Ernest and Calvin discuss the subject, and they both feel our election funding laws need major surgery, much along the lines Mr. Chavez proposes.

Calvin recalls that Mr. Chavez was the only congressional candidate in the primary who acknowledged Ernest. Perhaps he should have been a member of No Political Party (NPP).

We were now five months away from the November elections, and I wanted to inform the public of the growing support for their candidate. Our June 18 Friends of Ernest press release cited the most recent Red Dog Surveys poll as evidence of Ernest's high approval rating. Our survey results showed Ernest in the lead by a strong margin over all other candidates.

In the June 23, 1996 *Santa Cruz Sentinel*, in an article captioned "Dog-Gone Serious," staff writer Erin K. Quirk took note of the poll results. She wrote: "Ernest may run into some problems down the campaign trail, Shugart said, as California election law prohibits non-human candidates."

Describing Ernest as a "candidog," she informed her readers of my assurance that "the Friends of Ernest campaign will fight to the end."

A June editorial in the *San Francisco Chronicle* caught my attention and prompted my letter to the Editor, which was published in the July 3 *Chronicle*.

QUIET TIME THINKING

Editor—Your June 25 editorial, "It Takes A Private Moment," is right on. What has our political system become when a public figure can't admit contemplating the reaction of long gone public figures to current events, without a major event being forged.

I'm no great fan of Mrs. Clinton, but I think her quiet time thinking is valuable. I personally contemplate James Madison's reaction to the many constitutional issues facing us, when I have free thinking time.

Come on, you dirty laundry seekers, get a life.

While the letter wasn't directly related to Ernest or his campaign, it did reflect the adage, "Don't just do something, sit there!"

I try to take time out of my busy schedule to quietly reflect on what our Founding Fathers might have had in mind when they drafted certain Articles of the Constitution, what they might say or how they might act today, faced with the challenges of the twentieth century and a very different world. And often Ernest lies quietly by my side. Sometimes I even say aloud, "Ernest, what do you think about...?"

Ernest will look up with his big, brown eyes—eyes that often seem to say, "Right on, Al!" At other times they look more like, "What's this guy planning now?"

I was surprised when I received a flood of

# Friends of Ernest

ERNEST TAKES SURPRISING EARLY LEAD

*Calvin Reports Results Of Recent Poll*

PEBBLE BEACH, Calif.— June 18, 1996 — Ernest, an announced candidate for Congress from California's 17th District, was reported to have an 85% approval rating in a recent poll. The poll was conducted by Red Dog Surveys, according to Calvin, Friends of Ernest Treasurer.

Calvin presented statistics of a poll of 17th District voters who, when asked who they planned to vote for in the Congressional election in November, produced the following results:

| | |
|---|---|
| **Ernest** | **85%** |
| **Brown (Republican)** | **6%** |
| **Farr (Democrat)** | **6%** |
| **Others** | **3%** |

letters from people who voiced agreement with the letter. And a couple of long-lost friends tracked me down as a result of seeing it in the paper! That was a nice surprise.

On July 3rd I also wrote to Marv Rubinstein who had sent me a copy of his entertaining local (Carmel) newsletter, *The Affable Curmudgeon*. The summer, 1996, issue of Marv's eclectic news-humor-story-joke-book-review-political-commentary-and-editorial quarterly included this front-page dedication: "This issue is dedicated to ERNEST. I personally am voting for Clinton but, if any of you feel ambivalent, I suggest you vote for ERNEST." Prominently displayed on the back page was Ernest's campaign poster. In thanking Marv for his endorsement of Ernest for ambivalent voters, I included my subscription to his "Curmudgeon," which offers an enjoyable diversion.

The July 3 issue of the weekly *Carmel Pine Cone* offered additional entertainment. Joe Fitzpatrick mentioned my Seagate earnings in his column and added:

Anyway, old Alan really NEEDS that kind of cabbage this year because, as you know, he's running his dog, Ernest, for Congress and $6.2 million will finance quite a few TV spots. Not to mention some great Alpo fund raisers!

Now if he could just arrange a marriage for Ernest with Arianna Huffington's miniature poodle (she MUST have a miniature poodle), they could probably BUY the election!

Oh silly me—Arianna would never be party to trying to buy an election. And besides, Ernest (a Bernese Mountain Dog) may have an aversion to arranged marriages with miniature French poodles, as some other dogs do. (My Shih Tzu would start a tong war if I suggested such a thing.)

But good luck to Ernest and Al on their bizarre quest.

☆ ☆ ☆ ☆ ☆ ☆ ☆ ☆ ☆ ☆ ☆ ☆ ☆

# 7 July 17, 1996

# A Bureaucratic Leash And Muzzle

Sooner or later it was bound to happen. And it did. In July. The Federal Election Commission caught on: Ernest is a *dog!*

On July 17, 1996, John Gibson, FEC Assistant Staff Director, Reports Analysis Division, sent me a letter politely informing me that the FEC would no longer process our reports.

The FEC apparently had no idea until this date that Ernest was a canine candidate. Now they knew—and they weren't going to allow him candidate status.

This called for a press release! We informed the public of the FEC political maneuver. Then I sent Mr. Gibson a letter stating FOE would continue to file the required reports in an effort to establish Ernest's legitimacy.

Well, at least one person in Washington D.C. believed Ernest was a candidate. The President of Families Against Mandatory Minimums (FAMM), a national organization of individuals concerned about America's sentencing policies wrote to "Ernest Ernest." He offered him the greeting, "Dear

Congressional Candidate."

An enclosed survey sought candidates' views on current sentencing policies. Given the most recent FEC views on Ernest's candidacy, I opted for FAMM's alternative response: "If we do not hear from you, we will put "No Response" next to your name." So on FAMM's records, Ernest is among the "No Response" candidates.

Despite the FEC about-face regarding Ernest's legitimacy, people continued to write to Ernest and even include a contribution to his campaign. Among the letters of support was one from an attorney friend with a Santa Cruz law firm who let me know he was aware of my continuing efforts on behalf of Ernest and that his basset, Columbo, was available for assistance, if needed.

It was always encouraging to receive such letters.

Because I hadn't heard from the FEC regarding my request for information about any persons—other than the FEC—who might have questioned Ernest's candidacy, I sent another letter.

FEDERAL ELECTION COMMISSION
WASHINGTON, D.C. 20463

July 17, 1996

Alan F. Shugart
Friends of Ernest
P.O. Box 5908
Carmel, CA  93921

Identification No.  C00313130

Reference:  Letter to the Commission Dated June 24, 1996

Dear Mr. Shugart:

Thank you for responding to our Requests for Additional Information. Your response indicates that the candidate, Ernest, is a dog, which cannot be a candidate for Federal office. Although I do appreciate the humor involved in registering a dog as a candidate, the Federal Election Commission (FEC) will no longer be able to process any further reports or other information from "Calvin".

Staff resources are stretched very thin just attempting to process and review reports filed by the committees of legitimate candidates and filings from entities such as the Friends of Ernest only make the work more difficult and time consuming. I am sure you can appreciate the need to take this action. However, we will welcome any effort by you or Karen O'Connor-Seifert to become seriously involved in matters regulated by the FEC. If you have any questions, please contact Ginger Campbell on our toll-free number, (800) 424-9530 or locally at (202) 219-3580.

Sincerely,

John D. Gibson

John D. Gibson
Assistant Staff Director
Reports Analysis Division

cc:  Karen O'Connor-Seifert

# Friends of Ernest

## PRESS RELEASE

### ERNEST DECLARED ILLEGITIMATE BY FEDERAL ELECTION COMMISSION

*Calvin Advised Further Reports Will Not Be Processed*

SANTA CRUZ, Calif.—July 23, 1996 — At a hastily called campaign committee meeting, Ernest, an announced candidate for Congress from California's 17th District, disclosed that the Federal Election Commission (FEC) considers him to be illegitimate, and cannot be a candidate for federal office. Further, the FEC will no longer process reports from Calvin, Treasurer of Friends of Ernest (FOE), despite the fact that Ernest and FOE were issued campaign identification numbers in February, and two campaign finance reports had been accepted by the FEC.

Calvin, who has yet to finish law school, growled, "This is a constitutional issue on which the FEC has no right to rule. We will evidently be required to take the matter to the Judiciary."

Ernest, whose acceptance rating is 85% according to a recent poll, begged his supporters to hang in there until he and Calvin can get the matter resolved. Ernest suggested that dirty politics may have played a role in this turn of events, following nine months of successful campaigning.

The FEC Freedom of Information Act Officer contacted me on September 5, 1996, and I replied on September 12. This first request for information and a second follow-up request that I wrote in December, 1996, were finally answered on January 23, 1997, at which time Mr. Harris informed me that "A search of FEC records yielded no responsive documents to your Freedom of Information Act (FOIA) request." The correspondence between the FEC FOIA Officer and me was drawn out over several months.

The FEC had tried to send Ernest to the doghouse, but the press continued to regard him as a bona fide candidate and to inform the public about his progress. *The Bangkok Post* in Thailand reported the latest about Ernest in its August 4, 1996 edition. In a 3,500-word article, entitled, "The Thoughts of Chairman Al," the interviewer mentioned my being a "recovered golfer." (I did play a lot of golf, and I did quit.)

The writer quotes my thoughts about it: "If you spend too much time at anything, at work or at golf, it ruins your life. I have a broad range of things I like to do and keep a balance."

We discussed Ernest.

The writer asked me again about other things I do outside of Seagate. "My wife and I get involved in a lot of charitable things—the SPCA, AIDS research. We have a special education project to get underprivileged smart kids into private schools," I told him. "For a smart poor kid it's tough to get in. We feel strongly about a cause. Either you do it, or you don't. It's fun. If it's not fun, and you don't do good

for somebody, it's not worth doing."

And for me, Ernest's campaign is one of the things "worth doing."

Craig Zarley reported on Ernest's campaign in the August 26, 1996 *Computer Reseller News* advising readers, "there's more than just Ross Perot to keep us amused this political season. Enter Al Shugart's dog."

"Shugart admits that he would have preferred to run for office himself, but he's too busy running Seagate. So Al's best friend is the next best thing."

Zarley reiterated what had already been written—that my protest was more than "tongue-in-cheek chutzpah." It's to get people more interested in the political process and get rid of the bureaucracy.

My so-called "tongue-in-cheek chutzpah" inspired several more articles during the final months of the campaign. The weekend edition of the September 14-15 Singapore *Business Times* in its "Raffles Conversation" byline, published a lengthy article, "The Maverick in Al Shugart" by Kenneth James.

An introduction set the tone:

The story of Seagate president Alan Shugart is in many ways the story of the disk drive industry. And the creation of this unpredictable industry often involved giving the status quo a good shake-up. Kenneth James meets the man who, even today, isn't averse to thumbing his nose at convention.

James began:

In the hotel foyer where we have this Raffles Conversation, Al Shugart's shocking pink, short-sleeved batik shirt seems *au fait* with the casual gear of other tourists. His briefcase is another matter altogether. Prominently plastered on its weathered brown-leather top is a large US election campaign sticker with the legend: "Vote for Ernest." Ernest, the photograph plainly shows, is a dog.

To be exact, a three-year-old, 50-kg Bernese Mountain Dog. Ernest is a member of the Shugart family's large menagerie of pets. Up to late July, Ernest was also an announced candidate for the US Congress from California's 17th District.

"This is obviously a protest," Mr. Shugart explains. "The American public is getting apathetic towards the whole political system here, and the Republicans don't do anything, the Democrats don't do anything. So I was trying to create excitement by electing independents.

"We filed all the necessary papers with the Federal Election Commission, and they were very good, they gave Ernest a campaign number, they gave Friends of Ernest, which is the campaign committee, a campaign number. We've got (campaign) buttons, bumper stickers and posters. Ernest has been on the radio, TV, getting a lot of interest. People donated money. I've been turning in quarterly financial reports, how much we spent, how much we took in, which is not very much.

"Then all of a sudden three weeks ago the Federal Election Commission sent me a letter saying that Ernest is illegitimate, he can't be a candidate."

It won't be the end of the campaign, Mr. Shugart vows. "When the election is over, Friends of Ernest is going to stay in business as—pardon the pun—a citizens' watchdog group, to monitor those economic indicators that the government produces to find out how they get them. Because every attempt I've made so far, I've met with a stone wall. I'm not challenging the numbers. I just want to know how they got them."

# 8 September 22, 1996

# It's All About Common Sense

The following week, on September 22, 1996, a clever feature was published in the Sunday *San Francisco Examiner*. In his "Cyberspace" column, Technology Writer Tom Abate began writing about his interview with me, but ended up interviewing Ernest.

SEAGATE TOP DOG
BARKS UP POLITICAL TREE
   *PET MAKES NO BONES ABOUT WHO'S MASTERMINDING HIS RUN FOR CONGRESS*

Shugart breezed into his office at Seagate Technology Inc. wearing the Hawaiian shirt that's been his trademark since 1979, when he founded what has become the world's largest disk drive company.

Shugart had invited *The Examiner* to his headquarters in the Santa Cruz Mountains to meet Ernest. Ernest is a 3-year-old dog running as a write-in candidate for Congress, but Ernest was not around. He didn't like the long drive from the family residence in Pebble Beach, Shugart said.

So instead of talking to the most political animal since Emperor Caligula's horse. I listened to Shugart explain why he'd put $20,000 into a campaign kitty to finance the candidacy of a dog.

"I'm a total cynic with respect to politics," Shugart said. "I think the country is going to the dogs."

But I wondered if there was more to this story than a political stunt. What if the hound had wanted to sink his teeth into the issues, but had gotten muzzled instead? I could see the headline: Bowsergate.

But how could I get the scoop on Ernest if Shugart kept the pooch under wraps? My 7-year-old son provided the answer: Talk to the dog the way the other guy does. Use your imagination.

So employing the one technology Silicon Valley hasn't yet put on a chip, I met Ernest in the Cyberspace for a person-o-canine interview.

A muscular, 110-pound Bernese mountain dog, Ernest has a distinguished white swath running down his black underbelly. Patches of brown fur above his eyebrows made him look both wise and kind. Once I got used to his tongue lolling out while he listened to questions, I found him alert and surprisingly frank—for a politician.

*Examiner:* Whose idea was this candidacy?

*Ernest:* It was Al's. He put up the money. He wrote the press releases.

*Examiner:* Some might say you're just a puppet.

*Ernest:* Don't you think people are tired of political name-calling. The fact is I'm a dog. And I'm loyal. Al's been a good employer and a good friend. And he has lots of good ideas for the country. I'm proud to be his surrogate.

*Examiner:* Why doesn't Al just run himself?

*Ernest:* He thought about it when Leon Panetta resigned from Congress in 1992 to join the Clinton administration. He even had a slogan for his campaign buttons, "Al's your Pal."

*Examiner:* What happened?

*Ernest:* He decided it would have been irresponsible to jeopardize the livelihoods of the 90,000 people who work for Seagate to run for office.

*Examiner:* Plus he'd have to open up his finances and deal with reporters' questions. (The dog gave me a look.)

*Ernest:* I don't mind that he gets to do the talking. I'm a dog. It comes with the territory.

*Examiner:* But $20,000 seems like a lot to spend on a symbolic campaign.

*Ernest:* Not for Al. He contributed $250,000 to the campaign for the three initiatives in March. You know, the ones that would have set up no-fault auto insurance, limited attorneys' contingency fees and made it tougher to bring shareholder lawsuits. Unfortunately, all three initiatives lost. That's why I'm running for Congress — because Al is afraid people don't understand the danger.

*Examiner:* What danger?

*Ernest:* From the lawyers.

*Examiner:* The lawyers?

*Ernest:* The lawyers. Especially the ones who sue high-tech firms when their stocks go down. Al's been sued several times himself. You have no idea how mad it makes him. These lawyers are shaking down honest businesses while criminals run free.

*Examiner:* But didn't Congress just pass a bill to make share- holder lawsuits tougher to file?

*Ernest:* In federal court, yes. Clinton's lawyer friends pressured him to veto it, but Congress passed it anyway. But now the lawyers have an initiative on the November ballot to make shareholder suits easy in California. If the initiative passes, lawyers won't just sue companies. They'll go after the personal assets of board members. The best companies might flee California. That wouldn't leave you much to cover, would it, Mr. Technology Writer? I'm telling you, the lawyers could ruin Silicon Valley.

(I rub my chin.)

*Examiner:* Hmmm, this could be serious. But wait a second, don't Silicon Valley companies have patent attorneys?

*Ernest:* Of course. If companies couldn't protect inventions, they couldn't provide jobs or profits.

*Examiner:* I talk to a lot of copyright attorneys, too.

*Ernest:* Where would California's music, movie, and software industries be without them.

*Examiner:* And trademark attorneys?

*Ernest:* Look. No one denies the financial well-being of Silicon Valley depends on protecting intellectual property. What I'm saying is we can take some of the lawyers some of the time and other lawyers other times, but nobody can take all of the lawyers all of the time.

(Ernest rises up and bares his fangs.)

*Examiner:* Nice, Ernest. Good, Ernest.

(The growling subsides.)

*Examiner:* But isn't that a double standard?

*Ernest:* Not at all. Do you really think the leaders of Silicon Valley's top companies are

defrauding shareholders? Do you realize how much wealth these companies have created? These shareholder suits are just legal blackmail.

(I put down my notebook and pen.)

*Examiner:* Between me and you, if you're so upset at lawyers, why not chase their cars or poop on their lawns like a normal dog?

*Ernest:* That would make me feel better, but it won't help Al. And it won't help Silicon Valley. We're trying to make a statement.

*Examiner:* By running a dog for Congress?

(Ernest shakes his head.)

*Ernest:* That's just the kind of remark I'd expect from the media. You apparently have no appreciation for the long history of political satire. My advice to you is this: Just be grateful Al didn't have a pet snake.

During the weeks preceding the election, a few letters to Friends of Ernest trickled in, as did financial contributions. September 29, 1996 I received a note from my friend Tom Stafford, a former astronaut and retired Lt. General, and currently a business partner in a consulting firm in Washington. His sentiments are similar to those of many others who wrote about Washington politics:

*Dear Al,*

*After seeing the performance of the Congress, which just closed their session, I feel that Ernest could contribute a lot to the effort in Washington.*

*I am enclosing a check for $50.00 for his campaign. Please give Ernest my best and I hope he is successful in the campaign.*

*Sincerely,*
*Tom*

Barely three weeks away from the November elections, Friends of Ernest advised supporters that in spite of the refusal of officials to consider Ernest a bona fide candidate, surveys told the real tale: Voters were looking for an alternative at the polls, and Ernest was it.

When the *Monterey County Herald* published an editorial in favor of denying presidential Ross Perot the opportunity to debate along with candidates Dole and Clinton, I felt compelled to write this letter to the Editor. It ran September 27, 1996:

A QUESTION OF LOGIC
Let me see if I've got this right. We the taxpayers have given tens of millions of dollars to Clinton, Dole and Perot, and you are suggesting in your Sept. 20 editorial ("A debate without Perot") that it is proper for Clinton and Dole to keep Perot from the debates because he doesn't have a chance. If that kind of logic holds, then why did "we" give Perot $29 million? Perhaps what "we" should do is take a poll before any of our

# Friends of Ernest

## PRESS RELEASE

### ERNEST FACES MAJOR SETBACK

*Calvin Begs For Continuation*

SANTA CRUZ, Calif. — October 14, 1996 — Friends of Ernest (FOE) announced today that Ernest, an announced candidate for Congress from California's 17th Congressional District, has been denied write-in qualification by both Monterey and Santa Cruz Counties. Ernest, who immediately went into seclusion, declared this to be a continuation of California's disinterest in voters' concerns, when not even "None Of The Above" is allowed on the ballot or as a write-in.

Calvin, FOE Treasurer, barked instructions to campaign workers to continue the effort and encourage voters to write-in ERNEST. "While neither county will tabulate Ernest's votes, arrangements have been made with Red Dog Surveys to conduct an exit poll on election day to inform citizens of the real election results and the protest effect of a common sense candidate. It's unfortunate that the political bureaucracy would go to these lengths to keep an independent candidate with an 85% approval rating totally off the ballot."

money is distributed, and give it only to candidates with a chance.

I discussed this with my friend Ernest, who believes that the donation of our tax dollars to presidential campaigns is doggone stupid! Ernest growls that perhaps this problem will disappear when taxpayers quit marking the presidential election contribution box on their income tax returns.

Alan Shugart
Pebble Beach
*(Shugart notes that Ernest, a Bernese Mountain dog, is an announced candidate for Congress in the 17th District.)*

Four more political supporters sent Ernest letters in September. One letter from Minnetonka, Minnesota, enclosed a clipping from the *Lakeshore Weekly News* with a cartoon depicting a cat running for political office. The writer advised, "I'm sending you a cartoon from my local paper to make you aware that your campaign is being copy-CATted. Good Luck." Ernest sent his own reply and snorted that if cats are like "Mr. Whiskers" in the cartoon, well, they're pretty CATatonic.

A really nice tribute to Ernest, along with his photo, was published in the October, 1996 *Best Friends* magazine by the Best Friends Animal Sanctuary in Kanab, Utah. Estelle Gartenlaub sent me a copy. The article about Ernest concluded with these words:

We called Seagate and asked to speak to Mr. Shugart. "May I ask the nature of the call?" asked a lady who was obviously used to transferring calls to Customer Service.

"It's about Ernest's campaign. We want to know what qualifies him for high office."

"Mr. Shugart will be right with you."

"Ernest's prime qualification," Al told us when he came on the line, "is that he has no prior political experience."

I was always ready to talk about Ernest's campaign and the need for independent, nonpartisan thinkers. Usually people who called me at Seagate enjoyed the humor of Ernest's candidacy, but also appreciated the message underlying it.

Joe Fitzpatrick, in his October 24, 1996 *Carmel Pine Cone* column, didn't demonstrate his customary appreciation of Ernest's bid for public office. Usually amused and supportive, Joe now categorized the attempt to get Ernest on the ballot under the heading "These Foolish Things," and questioned the motivation behind the campaign. His conclusion: "I'm predicting that Ross Perot, Al Shugart's dog Ernest, and Mr. Ed will wind up in a dead heat! (Make that heap.)" At least Joe figured Ernest would get *some* votes!

In the October 6, 1996 edition of the San Jose area *Press Telegram*, columnist Catalina Ortiz discussed Silicon Valley voters' disillusionment with traditional party politics. The headline summed up local sentiment about the upcoming election: "Disgusted But Still Planning To Vote."

Ortiz cited as typical one local voter who "used to be interested in politics, enthusiastically supporting candidates and causes. Not anymore."

It was a symptom, Ortiz felt, of widespread "disgust with politicians and doubts about their ability to do much to solve society's problems."

She mentioned that Silicon Valley's independent spirit ran counter to the status quo: "A third party, or a candidate not beholden to any party, appeals to many voters here."

She concluded with some thoughts from Ernest—filtered through his campaign manager—to the effect that "campaign reform, principally limiting campaign spending, is necessary before a genuine independent can win high office. But that's just what the nation needs, he says."

The October 28, 1996 issue of *Fortune* magazine devoted a seven-page photo essay to man's best friend, portraying half a dozen company executives and their canine companions. Erik Calonius wrote the article and Timothy Greenfield was the photographer. (We used Greenfield's photograph of Ernest and me on the back cover of this book.) Erik had this to say about Ernest:

The most public of the lineup is Ernest, a Bernese mountain dog owned by Seagate Technology CEO Al Shugart. Ernest is running for the U.S. House of Representatives, from California's 17th District, and this is a serious matter to Shugart. He points out that, given the personal qualities of most politicians these days, Ernest's illiteracy and illegitimacy ought to be considered advantages.

☆ ☆ ☆ ☆ ☆ ☆ ☆ ☆ ☆ ☆ ☆ ☆ ☆

# 9 | November 5, 1996

# It's Not Over Till It's Over

November 5, 1996. Election Day. Seventeen months after Ernest's decision to run for office. Ten months after the official announcement of his candidacy. Even as voters filed in and out of precinct polling stations, Joe Fitzpatrick of the *Carmel Pine Cone*, tongue ever in cheek—and once again in Ernest's corner—penned these prescient words which appeared in print two days after the election:

> Right off the bat, you have to know that this column is being written Tuesday afternoon, a few hours before any election results are known.
>
> So if today's column seems more cowbrained than usual, it is probably because at this writing we don't know who won all those bellicose election contests, let alone which propositions survived.
>
> Still, the outcome of a few of the contests is so obvious even before the votes are counted that we have no qualms at all about commenting on how the results will affect our area.

Joe first offered his predictions and comments about presidential and assembly races, then had this to say about the local canine candidate (Joe must have seen the Red Dog Surveys Exit Poll figures):

> The only other contest in which we're certain of the outcome before the votes are counted is in the 17th Congressional District where Al Shugart's dog, Ernest, is certain to pull a major upset by walloping Sam Farr and Jess Brown!
>
> The big question, though, is what happens next? Does Ernest go back to Washington alone, or will Shugart accompany the pooch back there as exalted scooper, valet and interpreter on Ernest's staff?
>
> We worry about details like these.

Joe's question would be answered by statements from Ernest and Calvin after all the votes were counted and exit poll surveys completed.

A few days after the U.S. election, voters in Thailand went to the polls. Laurie Rosenthal, a writer for the Thai newspaper, *The Nation*, offered a few thoughts on Ernest in her "Pet Topics" column:

EARNEST ADVICE FROM A
DOGGIE POLITICIAN

As you prepare to vote today, perhaps you'd like to meet Ernest, who was involved in the recent United Stated elections.

This three-year-old Bernese mountain dog belongs to Al Shugart, who campaigned to put his dog on the November ballot for the US House of Representatives from California's 17th District.

Rosenthal recounted many of the campaign events recorded here, and added inside information for her Thai readers:

But don't start thinking that Shugart doesn't care about his dogs.

The chairman of Seagate Technology, the world's largest disk-drive manufacturer talks easily and knowledgeably about Ernest and Calvin, as well as the cats and six other dogs who live with him in Pebble Beach, California.

He does not love his dogs so much that he forgets that they are, after all, well, dogs. When his first grandchild was born last year, he had a dog trainer assess how much his animals could be trusted around a baby.

Ernest came out on top. "The trainer told me that he would trust Ernest anywhere, any time, in any situation, which is pretty much what I already thought," Shugart said.

And Rosenthal concluded:

Although he never actually ran in the US election, he continued campaigning right to the end, when he called for more voter participation.

Thai Radio followed up with a story about Ernest. I didn't hear the broadcast, but Seagate employees told me about it. I understand the newscasters got a real kick out of telling Ernest's story.

Around the same time, elections were being held in Australia, and producers from the biggest radio station there called me for an interview. They wanted to inject a spark into what most Australians considered to be pretty dull elections. They thought that news about Ernest's U.S. Congressional bid might do just that. Apparently it did. I heard that the Aussies had fun for a while tossing around the idea of a political race between a kangaroo and a crocodile.

I was in New York City around election time, and CNBC contacted me. They wanted the first-hand scoop about Ernest. And what a scoop! The challenger in the 17th Congressional District was not only an independent, and practically an unknown, he was also a dog! A real dog, of the four-legged persuasion. The CNBC TV and radio people must have had a good time reporting this piece of news. I have a hunch they were thinking, "It could only happen in California."

•

Ernest had fought the good fight. He never got his name on the ballot, but in the United States and on three continents his name was recognized as a symbol of protest. The elections over, it was now time to thank his

# Friends of Ernest

## PRESS RELEASE

### ERNEST CONCEDES ELECTION
*Citizens' Watchdog Activities To Continue*

SANTA CRUZ, Calif. — December 3, 1996 — Calvin, Treasurer of Friends of Ernest (FOE), announced today that Ernest has conceded the Congressional election in California's 17th District. "Exit poll data, taken by Red Dog Surveys, showed Ernest to have received an insufficient 2001 write-in votes, even though election officials declared that Ernest was not qualified and his write-in votes would not be counted. It's a doggone shame that a non-political candidate running on a platform of common sense can't be included in the election," barked Calvin to a pack of supporters. "With qualification and a bit of advertising we could have won the show," whined Calvin.

Ernest, accepting the results graciously as is his style, growled, "if they are not going to count my votes for Congress, I might as well have them not count my votes for Governor or President. I'll have to give that some more thought."

Both Ernest and Calvin made it perfectly clear that the citizens' watchdog activities of FOE will continue.

loyal supporters and look to the future. Amidst a large gathering of friends, on December 3, 1996, Ernest and Calvin informed the Media of their plans to continue the work begun through Friends of Ernest.

One more feature about Ernest appeared before year's end. On December 23, 1996, Mark Hachman published a fairly long profile of my years with Seagate in *Electronic Buyers' News*. Notable in this story is Hachman's assessment of what really makes for notoriety in the computer industry:

> Personally, Shugart's most notorious claim to fame is his dog, Ernest, who once staged a popular run at the House seat in California's 17th District. Originally planned as a satiric protest against inept politicians, Ernest gained a significant following before he was denied candidacy because he was ineligible to vote.

Well, there it is, in black and white: My claim to fame is Ernest!

So, a couple years from now somebody, somewhere, will mention Seagate Technology. And somebody else will say, "Oh, yeah. I heard about that Seagate guy whose dog ran for Congress."

"Yeah, Ernest. A Bernese Mountain Dog. And he had a sidekick. A basset."

"Yeah. Luther, or something like that."

"No. It was Calvin."

"That's right. Calvin."

And then somebody will say, "I sent Ernest's full-page ad to my sister in Yakima. She loved it. But what was the guy's name?"

"The guy? Beats me. I sure remember Ernest, though. That big pooch ran a tough campaign."

# Epilogue

From the time the ancient wolf first lowered his proud head and became companion to man, the dog has faithfully served those who respect and value his loyal service. Dogs have protected the hunter, guided the blind, been a hearing ear for the deaf, defended those in danger. They've saved the lives of soldiers and those sworn to protect the citizenry. Our dogs have brought us laughter by their playfulness, offered a quiet, listening ear for our secret hurts, filled our loneliness by their presence, made us better persons by their constancy. They have taught us about our own humanity—taught us how to be more human.

Throughout history, dogs have had a part in shaping the human story. The rigid form of a pet dog is forever preserved at Pompeii in the lava of Mount Vesuvius. Little dogs often graced the paintings of Jan van Eyck and Murillo, as symbols of love and faithfulness. Franklin D. Roosevelt's beloved Fala, enshrined in bronze, stands as tall as a little Scottie can beside the seated figure of his master.

Today dogs still play a prominent role in our public and private lives.

Millie, the springer spaniel, published her memoirs of a dog's life in the Bush White House.

Bosco, the elected mayor of Sunol, California, walked through his town, wagging his tail and greeting his constituents.

Abe Still's Graffin entered the 1996 presidential race, taking a stand on the troublesome issues of the day.

Josh, the spunky little 13-year-old mutt of Richard Stack of Maryland, also tossed his doggie collar into the 1996 presidential ring.

And of course, there's Ernest. Although he didn't win his congressional bid, he still campaigned right up to the end. He tried to be a voice for those looking for independent leaders. He sounded the alarm to rally dispirited voters to dismantle the systemic malignancy of ineffectual government. This was the core of Ernest's candidacy.

From the beginning I wasn't sure we could get him on the ballot. I thought that maybe in the beach-and-surfing community of Santa Cruz County we'd have a chance, even if we didn't in Monterey County. It wasn't to be. The answer simply was, "A dog can't run."

Election Day came and went. The percentage of eligible voters was way down. Ernest didn't seem to do much good. Maybe in the future he'll run again. I haven't given up on him yet. If a lot of people—beyond my immediate family and friends—buy this book, and if the pervasive disappointment with our government continues to grow, then maybe he'll again challenge the political status quo.

Today, no longer a candidate, Ernest remains an active watchdog. Joined by his Friends of Ernest "watchdog" group, Ernest still barks when the spirit and the letter of the United States Constitution is threatened and when our federal government acts in ways that are not in the best interests of the country. Friends of Ernest is now focusing on decisions made by tax-dollar-paid public officials, on actions that often leave us baffled, disbelieving, disgruntled, disgusted.

I had always wanted to find out about the numbers issued by the government. How do they get their statistical data? How many of us really know? How many of us take the information at face value, without questioning, without understanding—and, worse still, without caring? And we need to care. We are a government *of* the people.

Maybe Friends of Ernest can become a valuable protest group when things aren't going right. To date, FOE has been in contact with the Bureau of Labor Statistics, the Labor Department, the Census Bureau, the Conference Board (an information-gathering and data analysis agency under contract with the Government). FOE has requested information about statistics published by a number of Government offices, to find out how these figures are arrived at; for example the Consumer Price Index (CPI), and the Index of Leading Economic Indicators.

In some cases, Washington answers with vague, pre-packaged statements that don't address the specific queries. In other instances they say the information we request is "too complicated" to explain.

Far too often, agencies don't even bother to answer our letters.

We're not stupid. We deserve better. And we're growing wiser every day.

I believe Ernest has a future. People still ask about him. They hope he'll run again. Often when I'm being interviewed it's natural for me to say, "Well, I talked with Ernest about that..." or "Well, Ernest thinks..." He provides a vehicle for discussion. I still enjoy that.

Humor was a hallmark of Ernest's campaign. Humor will doubtless continue to characterize whatever Friends of Ernest pursues in the future.

Midway through Ernest's campaign I thought of creating a "Friends of Ernest" cartoon strip. I started looking around for an artist who could translate the Ernest concept into a visible, active, symbolic character. A number of people submitted material, but nothing clicked for me. Then my friend Jeff Whitmore suggested a local artist, Meg Biddle. Meg gave me some samples of her work, and I said, "This is it!"

Meg is clever and funny and a very talented artist. After we discussed the cartoon strip, she came up with some great sketches for Ernest and Calvin. She really captured them and brought them to life on paper. The strip evolved further to include "Clyde," the "infomaniac," "Edie," the little latchkey kid, and "Al."

I think this cast of characters lends itself to conveying the political and social goals that the Friends of Ernest watchdog group hopes to achieve.

# Ernest

**E**rnest was recently forced to resign his popular congressional campaign in California simply because he was a dog. Never mind the stacks of write-in votes and his clear, independent, common sense platform. Never mind his loyalty to his constituents and his flawless ethics. Never mind he was already housebroken.
Disappointed but not defeated, he's back as a political and social watchdog, sniffing out all the absurdities, follies, and fat with the help of his loyal supporters: Friends Of Ernest (F.O.E.).

# Al

**A**l shares a home with Ernest and Calvin. He's a relaxed kind of guy who works in the corporate world, but is not from there. His Hawaiian shirt is his badge of courage. Al shows up on lunch break to translate for Ernest when the need arises, especially when there are questions from the Press.

# Clyde

**C**lyde is a crow and a Deep Throat wannabe. He flies through congressional halls and past outdoor cafes collecting off-the-record, sometimes out of context information before getting run out with a broom.

# Calvin

**C**alvin is Ernest's best friend and advisor. He's a skeptical balance to Ernest's innocence. Calvin would say he's more grounded. So is his entire body due to the fact he's a 70lb basset hound

# Edie

**E**die is a spirited, politically savvy, little latchkey girl who befriends the two dogs on her way home one day. She not only understands Ernest, but considers him her equal and occasionally naps against his 110lbs of Bernese mountain dog fur for comfort and warmth.

## FRIENDS OF ERNEST • Al Shugart & Meg Biddle

If the cartoon strip is successful, and if this book finds a significant readership, maybe Ernest will continue to serve the people in his uniquely canine capacity.

People haven't forgotten Ernest. Not entirely anyway. This past December, 1997, over a year after the elections, I got a Christmas card from Tom McEnery, the former mayor of San Jose. It was addressed to "Alan Shugart & Candidate Dog."

Will people eventually forget about the Ernest campaign? Maybe not. William M. Vandiver, of Morrow, Georgia, urged Ernest to try again in a letter published in *The Santa Cruz County Sentinel* on July 12, 1997.

### TRY AGAIN ERNEST

While the election campaigns were in full swing I received a full page ad extracted from your paper exhorting the voters of California's 17th District to send Ernest to Washington, where he would serve as the United States Representative from the district (page A4, Jan. 11, 1996).

Unfortunately, the voters of the district did not see fit to rise to the challenge and support Ernest in his laudable quest. What a pity. A first class opportunity to bring fairness, honesty, ethics and common sense to government was lost. So you are now stuck with the same caliber of representation that the rest of us have.

And what about Ernest and his sidekick, Calvin. Rejected by the voters when offering outstanding representation was undoubtedly a severe blow to their egos, and it could not help but discourage attractive, potential candidates.

I hope Ernest can put this defeat behind him and again proffer his services in the 1998 elections. In recent years our country has had difficulty finding a few good men. Maybe a few good dogs could show us the way.

# Acknowledgements

As Friends of Ernest continued its efforts as a citizens watchdog group, Carmel Valley resident Marilyn Tully, the only paid member of FOE, took the time to put this book together. Marilyn has at least three other claims to fame: she is my wife's cousin; she's the daughter of Aunt Rose (at 93, probably the oldest loyal Friend of Ernest); and she shares her birthday with Ernest.

During the campaign my wife, Rita, and my Seagate assistant Karen Seifert, in spite of being convinced that I was some sort of nutcase, contributed their spare time enormously. Julie Still, also a Seagate employee, deserves our thanks for all her publicity assistance.

My son, Chris, who did most of the design of collateral material during the campaign, was always a strong supporter, and is the designer and editor of this book.

Meg Biddle deserves a special thanks for her collaboration on the Ernest comic strip. It's a political-social satire that has already found a home in several weekly newspapers.

There were many other "Friends"—too many, in fact, to list—but I do thank them all.

# Ernest Wants You!

## ...to be his friend

## Join Friends of Ernest

- Friends of Ernest is an accredited nonprofit and nonpartisan citizens watchdog organization founded in 1997. Our objective is to promote public interest in our government systems. (Like voting.)

- We believe in the Constitution and in getting it followed.

- We believe government facts and figures should be clear, not confusing. We study many kinds of information produced or sanctioned by the government for the purpose of making it easily understood.

- We report to FOE members with our findings because we believe citizens should have the opportunity to make informed decisions.

## JOIN NOW!

Membership is just $10.00 (Annual membership valid through 1999.) When you become a member, you will receive:

- Campaign button and bumper sticker.
- 8.5 x 11, black and white reproduction of the original campaign poster.
- Wallet-sized "Friend of Ernest card.
- Official FOE certificate.

Plus, you will receive special Friends of Ernest material such as newsletters, FOE updates, and important voter information as it's available.

---

Send check or money order to: Friends of Ernest, PO Box 5908, Carmel, CA 93921
Be sure to include your name and mailing address.